THE STARS WE KNOW

Oh, all you powerful beings above, look at me.
I want to be someone of consequence.
Give me long life and health.
Help me, protect me against any danger.
Oh gracious moon and stars,
I plead to you for help.

— Dawn Prayer of Two Leggings

THE STARS WE KNOW

CROW INDIAN ASTRONOMY AND LIFEWAYS

TIMOTHY P. McCLEARY

Little Big Horn College

WAVELAND
PRESS, INC.

Prospect Heights, Illinois

For information about this book, write or call:
Waveland Press, Inc.
P.O. Box 400
Prospect Heights, Illinois 60070
(847) 634-0081

To my son Austin Denny,

When the Twins returned to Earth they went back to their mother and she told them that the people in the sky were like birds, they could fly about as they pleased. Since the opening was made in the heavens, they may come down to Earth. If a person lives well on Earth, his spirit takes flight to the skies and is able to come back again and be reborn. A baby born with a dimple in the ear at the place where earrings are hung is such a reborn child from the people in the skies.

(as told by Arthur Mandan, Hidatsa Elder)

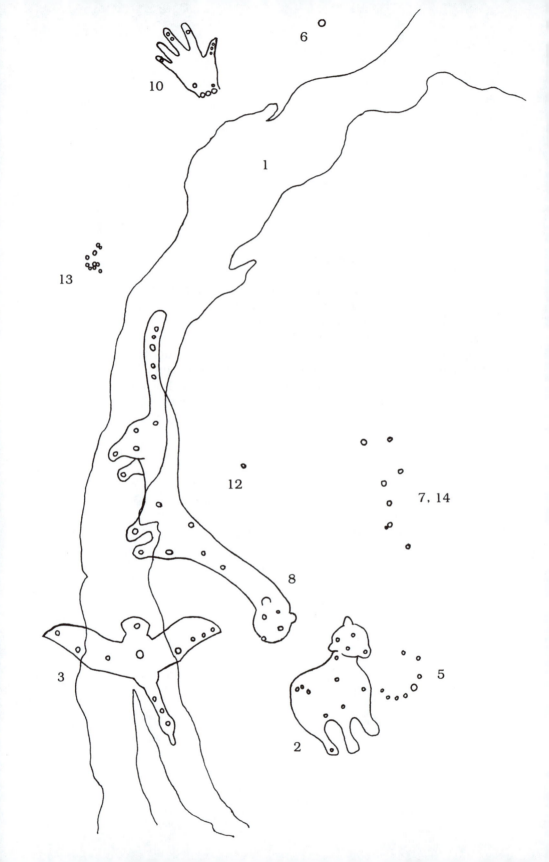

STARS AND CONSTELLATIONS
OF THE CROW

1. *Ammíaaalaau*
   Where They Take Women
   Milky Way

2. *Báakkaalaxpitchee*
   Bear Above
   Hercules

3. *Báakkaawiilee*
   Goose Above
   Cygnus

4. *Baappaaihké*
   Day Star (Evening Star)
   Venus (not pictured)

5. *Ihkaannáshe*
   Campsite Star
   Corona Borealis

6. *Ihkaléaxe*
   Bright Star (Morning Star)
   Sirius and planets

7. *Ihka Sáhpua*
   Seven Stars
   Big Dipper

8. *Ihkaúutte*
   Weasel Star
   Draco, Cepheus,
   Cassiopeia, Perseus

9. *Ihkawaaláaxe*
   Crazy Star
   Venus (not pictured)

10. *Ihkawaléische*
    Hand Star
    Orion

11. *Ihkawía/Ihkawilée*
    Woman Star/Fire Star
    Mars (not pictured)

12. *Ihkaxachíissee*
    Star That Does Not Move
    Polaris

13. *Ihkaxaxúa*
    Gathering of Stars
    Pleiades

14. *Iipchalapaachuoo*
    Pipe Pointer Stars
    Big Dipper

CONTENTS

FOREWORD

by Claire R. Farrer
California State University, Chico

Each of us grows up knowing that our own culture's ways of addressing and organizing life is the most sensible, if not the very best. That is simply part of the human condition. As we grow older and meet people from other countries or other cultures, either in person or through the educational process, we gradually learn that there are a vast number of ways of addressing and organizing life. Perhaps even more startling is that each of the ways seems to be as useful as any of the others. We may well quarrel with one group's predominant political organization or wonder how it happened that people we "know" to be relatives to each other do not consider themselves to be in terms of their own kinship system. It is the task of anthropology, the study of human beings and their myriad systems of organization, to present and make sensible the Others to Us.

Anthropologists take their task seriously, often spending years of their lives in other cultures, sometimes quite literally at the risk of their own well-being and health. The insights they glean about the tremendous variety of the human condition makes it all worthwhile, or so most of them believe. Rarely, there is a person like the author of this book, Timothy McCleary, an outsider who grew up with Others, learned their language as an adult, grew so close to people that they adopted him as one of their own, and who chooses to live among them throughout his life. It is a wonderful gift that in this book he shares some of his knowledge, learned from the Crow people, with those of us not so lucky to have had his experiences. Tim McCleary is the kind of anthropologist many wish to be.

There are many subspecialities within the discipline of anthropology. Some anthropologists spend most of their time with linguistics: the languages, grammars, lexicons, structures, and usage rules others have to communicate with one another. Some spend most of their time in laboratories, seeming for all the world like biologists as they strive to learn how and why we came to be as we are today. And some, quite recently, appear to have more in common with astronomers as they plumb the celestial vault. There are two kinds of these latter anthropologists: archaeoastronomers and ethnoastronomers. An archaeoastronomer uses the built environment and documents, where they exist, to learn about the astronomical systems of people and cultures no longer viable. By contrast, an ethnoastronomer works with living people, usually non-Western ones, who have an astronomical system that differs from that most Western people believe to be standard. It is in this latter area that the present book, *The Stars We Know*, falls.

Ethnoastronomers not only need to be able to spend long hours outside at night when others are snuggled down under quilts, but also they must have established a special rapport, or relationship of trust, with those from whom they learn. In many Indian tribes, ethnoastronomical knowledge is highly specialized and not necessarily shared among everyone within the tribe. Among other tribes, such knowledge is available to any tribal member who is interested. And among many tribes there are several versions of sky knowledge extant at any one time; while this is bothersome to Westerners, who believe there is only *one* truth, it is known among Native American people that Creator's knowledge is so vast that we mere humans glimpse only a portion of it at a time. Therefore, several versions or visions of the sky are all equally plausible and probably all equally true. No matter the specific beliefs of any one particular group of people, star knowledge is seldom shared with outsiders. So this book joins the ranks of only a few others devoted to the astronomy of Native people of the Americas.

One of the first book-length treatments of Native North Americans was done in 1978 by Travis Hudson and Ernest Underhay, *Crystals in the Sky: An Intellectual Odyssey Involving Chumash Astronomy, Cosmology, and Rock Art* (published by Ballena Press.) Because the California Chumash were so decimated during the Spanish colonial period, this work is not true ethnoastronomy but rather is somewhere between ethno- and archaeoastronomy.

Another book that spans the two subdisciplines is Ray A. Williamson's *Living the Sky: The Cosmos of the American Indian* (published by Houghton Mifflin Company in 1984); this book looks at all of Indian North America, but emphasizes the American Southwest.

Williamson and Farrer (University of New Mexico Press, 1992) brought together several scholars who were concerned with ethnoastronomy in *Earth and Sky: Visions of the Cosmos in Native American Folklore*. Most of the information in this book was from first-hand sources, but some of it came through documents and educated guesses.

Ronald Goodman's book, *Lakota Star Knowledge: Studies in Lakota Stellar Theology* (second edition printed by Sinte Gleska University in 1992), is truly ethnoastronomy as it was compiled with a group of Lakota people as a part of the research that was done for their land claims case against the United States government. However, the project soon took on a life of its own and became an end in itself.

Trudy Griffin-Pierce, herself part Catawba Indian, was adopted into a Navajo family upon the death of her own mother. Through her interests in art and Navajo ways, she gradually came to an appreciation of the relationship between ethnoastronomy and dry-paintings, or sandpaintings. However, the knowledge she sought and was learning is dangerous and so her Navajo relatives arranged to have a "sing," a blessing and curing ceremony, performed for her to protect her as she pursued her work. You may read of her work in *Earth Is My Mother, Sky Is My Father: Space, Time, and Astronomy in Navajo Sandpainting* (published by the University of New Mexico Press in 1992).

Dennis and Barbara Tedlock, a husband-wife team, have worked with both the Zuni people of the American Southwest and the Highland Maya people of Guatemala. Most of their ethnoastronomical work appears in advanced, scholarly outlets, but Barbara's *Time and the Highland Maya* (published by the University of New Mexico Press in 1982 with a revised edition published in 1992) is accessible to those who are just becoming interested in the topic.

Gary Urton works in South America; his *At The Crossroads of the Earth and the Sky: An Andean Cosmology* (published by the University of Texas Press in 1981) has fascinated many readers because of his description of the custom of using the dark spaces in the celestial vault as "constellations."

Stephen Michael Fabian also works in South America; his *Space-Time of the Bororo of Brazil* (University Press of Florida, 1992) integrates the sky with everyday life of a group of Brazilian Indians.

Using an artifact, a painted buckskin star chart, and the writings of anthropologists from the last century, Western astronomer, Von Del Chamberlain, was able to reconstruct some of the astronomical system of Pawnee people in *When the Stars Came Down to Earth: Cosmology of the Skidi Pawnee Indians of North America* (Ballena Press, 1982).

Finally, my own *Living Life's Circle: Mescalero Apache Cosmovision* (University of New Mexico Press, 1991) attempts to place ethnoastronomy centrally in life, as indeed the Mescalero Apaches know it to be.

But why such interest? Isn't the sky the same everywhere? It is precisely because the sky appears different from particular places on the globe that astronomers and anthropologists work with each other in this subdiscipline of anthropology. The stars that can be seen on any given night of the year vary, depending upon whether one's vantage point is the North Pole, the South Pole, the Equator, and indeed scores of places in between. Even when restricting the vision just to North America, there is tremendous variation in what can be seen. So called naked-eye astronomy, what can be seen with one's eyes, is the kind of astronomy practiced by the Native people of North America. This means not just the sun and stars, but also planets, comets, meteors, and the moon were watched.

Sometimes the watching was to construct a calendar. The stars and constellations seem to become visible a little earlier each night of a solar, or sun, year—the time it takes for the earth to make one full revolution around the sun. To our eyes, the sun seems to be orbiting the earth, since it rises and sets in different positions on the horizon throughout the course of a year. So, throughout the course of the year, the constellations and stars change in relation to a person watching from the same place each night. Even though the difference in rise time is only about four minutes in one twenty-four hour period, the accumulation means that in one lunar cycle, one month, the difference has reached two hours. This occurs because the stars' apparent movement is four minutes longer than the sun's journeying. By the time a quarter of the year has passed, there is a six hour difference. Taken through the course of a year, it accounts for the sun's position and what we normally term "the stars of summer," or any other season; stars that appear just after sunset in the east or south or west or north will have shifted their positions 90° by autumn, another 90° by winter, and yet another 90° by spring, returning to their summer positions at the end of that year. These predictable shifts correspond to the seasons mid-latitude people experience. By watching when the stars and constellations first appear after sunset in the east (or any other direction), it is easy to construct a calendar.

It is trickier to make a calendar using the moon, since its cycle of waxing, waning, and disappearing takes 29 1/2 days. Using the moon's position among the stars makes a tricky situation even tougher, since it takes only 27 1/3 days for the moon to be at a given position with respect to the stars and return to that same position. Obviously the phases of the moon and its position among the stars do not have a one-to-one correspondence with each other. And equally obvious by simple division, neither moon cycle maps very well onto the solar one. If people choose to set a calendar with the moon, then every three years or so they have to add a month to make the moon and sun work together properly again. There are other ways to work out the relationship as well, none of them particularly easy or very intellectually appealing. So Native Indian people had to make adjustments in order to make what they saw consistent with the various cycles that are easily observed with one's eyes.

The consistency is often kept in narratives. Sometimes the narratives are myths, sacred narratives; it is these that are difficult for outsiders to learn about, for it requires a suspension of one's own beliefs in order to inaugurate belief in another system so that understanding can occur. Often, too, it is the myths that are the charter of only a few specially trained individuals in a culture. The odds of an anthropologist being accepted by such individuals are slim indeed and partially account for there being so few books like McCleary's. Sometimes the narratives are cast into legend form where a person, believed or known to have existed, sets out the rules and signs by which people can recognize seasons or shifts that are about to occur in the sky. Or the narratives can be in what are usually called folktales, narratives in which magical people and events have a place. No matter the form the narratives take, each encodes important information about the sky and how people should properly live beneath it.

Dale Old Horn, in the Prologue to this book, indicates that the cosmos is known and organized by Crow people and is taught to their children. He speaks of the holiness of prayer addressed to Creator, of the unity of all creation, of the awe and reverence with which his people conceive of the cosmos and all within it, and of the power that resides in the celestial vault. And he speaks of the poignant, of how becoming educated in the Western way threatens to destroy the unity of the Crow way. He knows books like the one you are about to read will help keep the destruction at bay.

Timothy McCleary is privileged to be trusted by Crow people. He knows this and respects it. There is much more he could tell than what he has written between the covers of this book. But the respect he accords to Crow people and traditions mandates that he tell only that which he was given permission to tell. It is partly for that reason that Dale Old Horn writes here, too—to tell each of you that what you are about to learn is holy, sacred, and that it is now the time to share some of it.

PROLOGUE

The Crow people believe that all creation is of *Iichíhkbaalee*, First Maker, our Creator. No part of creation exists outside of First Maker's realm. And since everything exists because of this creation then nothing is excluded. The Crow Indians' understanding of creation and the vastness of the cosmos was demonstrated to me when I was a child.

Many times I had the distinct privilege and blessing of listening to my maternal great-grandmother, *Baaxpáash*, "One Who Is Sacred," pray at sunrise. She would say, "Creator, You who created all things. You who created things that we can see and things we will never see. You who created things that we can understand and things we will never understand." This prayer showed me the magnitude of the creation of *Iichíhkbaalee*.

Since all things come from the Creator, the Crow Indians also believe that the power from First Maker permeates all things. This is why the Crow believe in intercessory spirits or agents of the Creator. So for the Crow it is not unusual to say and believe that everything has a soul or spirit. This belief further states that the Creator's power is shown and given to fortunate blessed individuals through seven entities: the heavens, air, fire, earth, water, plants, and creatures.

The power that is in the heavens includes the sun, which is called the "Old Man," *Isáahkaxaalia*; the moon, which is called the "Old Woman," *Káalixaalia*; and the stars, *Ihké*. The Old Man is believed to be the center of wisdom, while the Old Woman is believed to have the power over conception and livelihood.

For the Crow all the stars are sacred. Within our cosmogony and cosmology, however, there are constellations that have special religious interpretation and history. One constellation that is always prominent in our lifeways is the Big Dipper. It is termed *Ihka Sáhpua*, "Seven Stars," and also *Iipchalapaachuoo*, "The Place Where The Pipe Is Pointed." This constellation is also the place where the "Seven Sacred Brothers," *Akbachakúpe Sáhpua*, the "Seven Sacred Bulls," *Bishée Chíilape Sáhpua*, and the "Seven Sacred Rams," *Iisaxpúatahche Sáhpua* reside.

The power of air is found in the wind, the clouds, and in thunder and lightning. The sacredness of water is found in rivers, springs, and lakes, and it is also found in what is called *báakkaawile*, "above water"—snow, sleet, hail, rain, and mist. When the Crow speak of creatures, *baaisbiláaleete*, "those without fire," they include all that move of their own volition—reptiles, birds, amphibians, mammals, fish, and everything else that moves on its own accord.

The teachings of these seven entities (the heavens, air, fire, earth, water, plants, and creatures) provide the basis of our beliefs. Their precepts have shaped the innate understandings of Crow nationhood. They have become the guiding force of an entire lifeway, providing our sense of right and wrong and our attendant sense of values and ethics.

Once the Crow nation had strength, beauty, and a strong sense of national identification. Today, however, we see a demise in this cultural heritage. The use of the Crow language is waning, and there are groups—even amongst the Crow people—who decry the validity of native spirituality. The rich resources of the Crow are being exploited by non-Indians and we are poverty stricken—so much so that the majority of the Crows must rely on public assistance. It is hard to have an elevated sense of intellectual realization when we are hungry. This condition has led to despair and defeatism.

It is through intellectual curiosity and the acquisition of knowledge that our negative self-concepts can be replaced. Scholarly research and writings, such as seen in this book, can have a very positive impact on the Crow, both within and outside the reservation. This book on our traditions related to the heavens expresses a part of the native theology of the Crow in a careful, thoughtful, and detailed manner. From this, the native culture is much better understood both by Crow people and by non-Indians. I believe this inevitably will lead to improved self-awareness, which strengthens group and cultural interaction, ensuring the future of the Crows as a people and as a part of *Iichíhkbaalee*'s beautiful creation.

Dale D. Old Horn
Little Big Horn College

ACKNOWLEDGMENTS

I thank the many people and institutions that provided assistance and cooperation during this project. I am grateful to the families of Guy and Eloise White Clay, who accepted me as a son. Through this act of graciousness and affection Guy and Eloise not only provided me with a Crow name (*Baaxpáash*, Holy) and lineage (White Clay and Tobacco), but also clan relations (Big Lodge member/Ties the Bundle child), historic political band division (River Crow), and reservation district (Black Lodge). It is with great pride and appreciation that I accept and defend all these new roles. *Ahó kaashiilaa*.

Elders who contributed knowledge and time include Barney Old Coyote Jr., Mickey Old Coyote, Grant Bulltail, George Reed Jr., William Gros Ventre, Francis Stewart, Dan Old Elk Sr., Kenneth Spint, Leroy White, Vincent Goes Ahead, Winona Plenty Hoops, Lillian Hogan, Alma Snell, and Sylvia Stops. To these special contributors. *Ahó kaashiilaa*.

A sincere thanks to Dale Old Horn, Department Head of Crow and Social Studies at Little Big Horn College. He is a preeminent cultural historian, genuine scholar, and vital friend. Through many discussions on native/contemporary Crow culture, he has sharpened my intellectual skills and understanding. As a scholar and a friend he has been extremely helpful throughout this project. *Ahó kaashiilaa*.

A special thanks to Magdalene Moccasin, my coworker and assistant in this project. She provided much of the preliminary work: searching out potential interviewees, setting up interviews, and, in many cases, doing the interviews. She also located transcribers and translators. She was particularly instrumental in locating elders without whose contribution this project would not be complete. To my friend and colleague. *Ahó kaashiilaa*.

Little Big Horn College Library staff have been helpful and expedient in locating often obscure materials that have provided a foundation of Crow and native star knowledge. To Chief Librarian Timothy Bernardis and Assistant Librarian Carson Walks Over Ice. *Ahó kaashiilaa.*

The primary translators and transcribers were Belva Tushka and Kathy Old Horn. The typed transcriptions were then entered into a word processing program by Lou Old Coyote, Carie Chasing Hawk, Christina Hill-Stops, and Michelle Bird. Crow linguistic and translation issues were clarified by Dale Old Horn and Euna Rose He Does It. Lida Bear's Tail, Martha Baker, and Gerard Baker provided Hidatsa linguistic and cultural information. Monies to pay consultants were provided by a special Little Big Horn College allocation through President Janine Pease-Pretty On Top and a National Science Foundation grant administered by Bob Madsen. Dennie Carlson and Tim Anderson provided comments on early editions of the manuscript. To these contributors and consultants. *Ahó kaashiilaa.*

Thanks to Peter Nabokov, my elder in the field of anthropology and Crow Indian research. He has provided much insight and a fine tuning to this document that only a person of his intellect and experience could have provided. To my elder brother in the field. *Ahó kaashiilaa.*

Thanks to Doug Kuhlman for taking photographs and providing access to his collection of photos of the Crow people and their reservation. He refuses to accept payment for these photos, since, as he says, "I'm their guest." So all he has received for the photos included here is a courtesy line and this thanks. *Ahó kaashiilaa.*

A thanks to Dr. Barney Old Coyote, who not only contributed knowledge to this work, but also continues to be a special elder to me. He has patiently guided me through parts of Crow culture which are often lost on an outsider. *Ahó kaashiilaa.*

Thanks to Claire R. Farrer who provided comments and, through several lengthy phone calls, encouragement and praise. She also provided editorial advice as well as the foreword and study guide. Above all other contributions, however, she sought and made the initial contacts with a publisher. Claire's total contribution to the final product cannot be overemphasized. To my elder sister in arms. *Ahó kaashiilaa.*

Last but not least, a special thanks to my wife, Carrie, who is the mother of my children, Austin Denny and Katherine Nova, the bright stars of my days and nights. Carrie has remained my strongest supporter throughout this research. She has backed and encouraged this work as no other. It is to my companion and friend that I say a special *ahó kaashiilaa.*

Timothy P. McCleary
Star Route
Two Leggings, Montana

CROW LANGUAGE ALPHABET AND PRONUNCIATION GUIDE

The Crow Bilingual Materials Development Center has developed an alphabet for writing the Crow language, and all Crow words in this document utilize this alphabetical system.

The Crow alphabet is composed of twenty-seven characters:

a aa b ch d e ee h i ii ia k l m n o oo p s sh t u uu ua w x ?

Crow vowel qualities are:

a	*a*vailable
aa	f*a*ther
e	b*e*t
ee	*a*ble
i	b*i*t
ii	b*ea*t
o	st*o*ry
oo	ab*o*de
u	p*u*t
uu	b*oo*ed
ia	ar*ea*
ua	Nash*ua*

Crow consonant qualities are:

b	*b*ed
ch	*ch*urch (at the beginning or end of a word)
ch	*j*ail (when between vowels)
d	*d*og

h	*h*alf
k	*k*itchen (at beginning or end of a word and when doubled within a word)
k	*g*uy (when the letter k appears between vowels)
l	*l*eap (a sharper "l" than in English)
m	*m*an
n	*n*ot
p	*p*aper (at beginning of a word and when doubled within a word)
p	*b*aby (between vowels)
s	*s*ize (at beginning of a word or when doubled within a word)
s	*z*oo (when between vowels)
sh	*sh*oe (at the beginning or end of a word)
sh	plea*s*ure (when between vowels)
t	*t*ime (at beginning of a word or when doubled within a word)
t	*d*ay (when between vowels)
w	*w*ay
x	*acht* (German ch)
?	uh-oh (glottal stop)

Almost all Crow words have a vowel that is stressed. The stressed vowel is indicated by an accent mark. The accent is essential for meaning, pronunciation, and spelling. In most cases, the word does not have meaning without the accent. For example, "ahpe" is not a word, but *áhpe* means "evening" while *ahpé* means "his/her ear."

Also, when referring to a proper noun, Crow people add a *sh* sound. The *sh* is not added when speaking directly to the person. Therefore, proper nouns spelled in Crow appear with a *sh* ending in reference and without in address.

Chapter 1

OUR SIDE

This book is intended to provide insight into a little known aspect of Crow culture—Crow ethnoastronomy. Ethnoastronomy, a fairly recent development in the human sciences, attempts to elicit how non-Western peoples' perceptions of cosmic phenomena are utilized in structuring behaviors, values, and mores (Williamson and Farrer 1992:279–80).

The initial motivation for this project came from the desire to provide Crow students at the tribally controlled college, Little Big Horn College, with information on how Crow people view and interact with the cosmos, to show them that their culture's view of the world is as valid as that of the Euro-American. The Crow Astronomy Project, as it became known, started in the fall of 1993 and continued into the spring of 1996. An earlier version of this document was supplied to the bilingual program on the reservation and has been utilized in courses at Little Big Horn College.

The Crow people of southeastern Montana formally call themselves *Apsáalooke*, which translates as "Children Of The Large Beaked Bird." This term was erroneously translated as "Crow" by early Europeans and has since been their English name. Informally, however, the Crow call themselves *Bíiluuke*, which translates as "Our Side." To be *Bíiluuke* implies not only common genetic ances-

1

Dale Old Horn speaking at the Little Big Horn College 1995 commencement exercises (photo by Doug Kuhlman).

try, but, more importantly, common language, religious beliefs, and social structure.

Contemporary Crow Indians are descendants of nomadic hunters and warriors. Their ancestors lived in tipis, moved about the Great Plains in search of game, primarily buffalo, and fought intertribal battles over honors and horses. In past times the Crow people followed a generalized yearly pattern. Small family groups in the winter would gather into larger kin-based groups in the spring to harvest edible roots. As summer approached, they gathered into their respective bands, or possibly, even the whole tribe, for large buffalo hunts. Fall brought a return to smaller groups to pick berries and then a break into family or kin groups again for the winter.

Historically, the Crow people recognized three political divisions. The largest of these was known as the *Ashalahó*, "Where There Are Many Lodges," or the Mountain Crows, who lived in northern Wyoming and southern Montana, ranging as far east as the Powder River and west as far as Livingston, Montana. The second largest was the *Binnéessiippeele*, "Those Who Live Amongst The River Banks." This division ranged from the Yellowstone River, in the south, to the Milk River, in the north. The last division of the Crows was known as the *Ammitaalasshé*, "Home Away From The Center," or, more commonly, *Eelalapíio*, the "Kicked In The Bellies," because a member of this band was kicked by a colt when the Crows first encountered horses. This division derived from the Mountain Crow band. They became a distinct division because of their habit of spending the winters in the Wind River country of southwestern Wyoming and summers on the eastern side of the Big Horn Mountains in Wyoming and Montana, on the fringe or away from the center of the Crow world.

The three groups, Mountain, River, and Kicked In The Bellies, consisted of several individual villages, or sub-bands. During most of the year, especially winter, these villages remained independent and scattered about the respective territories of each band. But for special occasions, such as the planting of Sacred Tobacco, Sun Dances, or a fall buffalo hunt, the various villages would come together as one band and, occasionally, as one nation.

The force which most strongly influenced the gathering of Crow people was the availability of game and edible plants. Beginning in the spring, the Crow people would gather in larger and larger groups until the early fall buffalo hunt. This was possible because of the availability of roots, berries, and game in spring and summer. After the fall buffalo hunt, the large groups, sometimes comprising the whole tribe, would break into small groups. These small groups would seek sheltered areas in which to spend the winter. The tribe would break into these smaller groups because of the decrease in available game. In fact, these winter groups often relied on stored food—dried meat, roots, and berries—that had been procured and processed during the summer.

Today the Crow reservation, formed at the turn of the century, is a mere 2.2 million acres, compared to the estimated 38 million acres they once controlled. On this reservation are six districts and six major towns (see map on next page). The reservation is cut by two major rivers, the Big Horn and its tributary the Little Big Horn, which run south to north. These rivers create two major valleys and the natural divisions between the three mountainous areas on the reservation, the Pryors, Big Horns, and Wolf Mountains. In the northern districts of Black Lodge and Reno, and in the upper parts of the Big Horn and Pryor Districts, the terrain is open rolling hills interrupted only by cottonwood trees and brush that line river and creek beds. These open lands are used for high-quality winter wheat and sugar beet agriculture. The gently rising mountain ranges on the southern half of the reservation are covered in cedar and jack pine where elk, mule deer, and black bears are often seen. The mountains remain a vital resource to Crow people for food, medicines, and spiritual retreat.

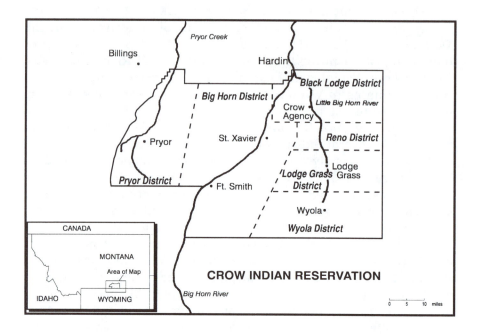

The six towns of the reservation are dominated by govern-ment-built housing developments, what are referred to as "housings" by Crow people. Crow Agency, the town in which the federal and tribal government offices are located, is some fifty-seven miles east of the city of Billings. Near or in this community are the Indian Health Service hospital, the tribally controlled college, and the site of Custer's last stand, Little Bighorn Battlefield National Monument.

South of Crow Agency is the major reservation town of Lodge Grass, in the district of Lodge Grass. This typical western ranch community is built on the bottom lands of the Little Big Horn River. To the west, over the foothills of the Big Horn Mountains, is the town of St. Xavier in the Big Horn District. In this community are a one-hundred-year-old Catholic mission and school which are sur-rounded by a handful of homes. South of St. Xavier, along the Big Horn River, is the growing community of Ft. Smith. This town is built on the historic site of a fort that guarded the Bozeman Trail for a brief period in the 1860s. After the construction of the Yellowtail Dam in the 1960s, the town swelled with an influx of out-of-state fish-ermen seeking a chance at the trophy-size trout that grow in the cold after-dam waters.

To the west of Ft. Smith lies the isolated hamlet of Pryor. Nes-tled against the pine-covered Pryor Mountains, this small com-munity, known as a bastion of Mountain Crow traditions, is inviting

Terrain typical of the Crow Reservation—open flat lands with tree-lined rivers and creeks and gently rising escarpments, Lodge Grass District (photo by Doug Kuhlman).

and friendly. This town was the residence of the last Crow chief, Chief Plenty Coups, and his home, now a Montana State Monument, was preserved by the chief's wishes for all peoples.

The three political divisions of the Crow settled in separate areas on this reservation. Descendants of the Mountain Crow can be found in the central and western parts of the reservation, in the Big Horn and Pryor Districts. The descendants of the River Crow can be found in the northern part of the reservation, in the Black Lodge and Reno Districts. The Kicked In The Bellies are located on the eastern side of the reservation, in the districts of Lodge Grass and Wyola.

To a large extent the family, village, and band wanderings of the historic Crow have been retained in family, district, and tribal activities of the reservation. In winter, families cloister to their homes

In the Big Horn Mountains, southern Big Horn District (photo by Doug Kuhlman).

in towns and ranches across the reservation, and the family listens to an elder tell stories or simply watches television. Beginning in spring, districts gather for hand-game tournaments and special dances, followed by summer district pow-wows and rodeos, followed by the large intra- and intertribal gathering of Crow Fair in late August, corresponding to the former fall buffalo hunt. In fall, activity slows and families return to a more sedentary lifestyle in preparation for winter.

The contemporary Crow people also continue to maintain their language and beliefs despite the economic and cultural oppression they have faced for the last one hundred years. Most Crow people are bilingual, however many prefer to speak their native language and follow Crow customs and beliefs. They practice a complex kinship system which has different expectations for those on the mother's side than for those on the father's side. The mother's relatives are expected to provide for the emotional and physical needs of the individual, whereas the father's side is expected to provide the religious training and social recognition of the individual.

"Clan fathers" and "clan mothers," as those on the father's side are called, are highly respected and sought for a variety of social and religious needs. Individuals in this standing are expected to provide advice, prayers, and religious instruction for their "clan children." This relationship can be seen as the basis of Crow social and religious structure, since everybody is a clan father or clan mother to someone.

When Crow people are asked what religion they follow, they often respond by identifying themselves with a Christian group, such as Baptist, Catholic, or Pentecostal. Most Crow people, however, continue to follow native beliefs and practices. Even the most devote Pentecostal has difficulty ignoring clan father or clan mother responsibilities.

The clan fathers and clan mothers are therefore the ones who transmit the moral, ethical, and behavioral expectations of Crow cul-

Horse racing at Crow Fair, 1995 (photo by Doug Kuhlman).

Miss Crow Fair, second from right, and District Princesses at Crow Tribal Rodeo Grounds, Crow Fair 1995 (photo by Doug Kuhlman).

ture. This instruction is generally conveyed through narratives, and stars often play a central role in these stories. The stars, as well as other celestial phenomena, are a major component of Crow moral and ethical precepts.

When visiting the Crow Indian Reservation in Montana, the area which is regionally called the Big Sky Country, it is easy to understand why and how the stars became important to Crow people. The natural beauty of Crow Country is only rivaled by the vast expanse of sky overhead. The clear night skies reveal a bowl of stars shining brightly overhead, yet also dancing close to the ground. This quality of the Montana night has taken on metaphorical significance for the Crow people, who express the concept of quiet peace or serenity with the phrase *ihkaxáaxaaheetak*—"the stars are shining brightly." As one elder stated, "When all was quiet in the camps and peace was about, no inclement weather, then people were wont to say, '*ihkaxáax-aaheete, ahó, ahó*,' the stars are brilliant tonight, thanks, thanks."

However, the intimate connection of their star knowledge to other sacred beliefs and practices of the Crow people made it initially difficult for me to gather information on the subject. It was

The Crow Indian Reservation's location in a region known as Big Sky Country makes it easy to understand how the stars became important to the Crow people (photo by Doug Kuhlman).

often confusing to Crow elders how or why stars or other celestial phenomena would be considered apart from their interconnectedness with the rest of the natural and spiritual world. In fact, it eventually became apparent that the two should not nor could not be separated. This book, therefore, is more than a description of Crow star knowledge. It is a description of Crow cosmo*gony*, or the stories of the origins and organization of the universe, and Crow cosmo*logy*, or the beliefs and philosophies about the universe. Recently, these two concepts have been merged by ethnoastronomers into the single term *cosmovision* (Williamson and Farrer 1992:280). Therefore, this book can be considered a presentation of the Crow cosmovision, the very essence of ethnoastronomy.

An informal interview pattern was utilized to gather this contemporary information on Crow ethnoastronomy. Questions were asked of each elder and then he or she was allowed to elaborate freely. The majority of the interviews were conducted by myself and Little Big Horn College archivist, Magdalene Moccasin. Occasionally, a student at the college interviewed a relative or a friend. Whenever possible, the interviews were conducted in the Crow language and then translated and transcribed. Copies of the taped interviews have been deposited in the Little Big Horn College Archives.

When narratives were recorded in the Crow language, the translations were reviewed with a second and sometimes third Crow speaker to ensure that nuances of meaning were not lost and to maintain as much of the Crow oral performance style as possible. Some narratives were recorded in English. These narratives were usually transcribed verbatim so that the voice of the elder could come through. I have retained as much of these voices in the text as possible, to conserve the meaning and flavor of Crow oral traditions. Sometimes minimal editing was necessary for clarity in English.

Crow storytelling and cultural training is passed on during winter evenings. Historically, the timing of Crow stories served a practical purpose, to entertain during the long winter nights while the fire was tended. In this manner, the household would be kept warm throughout the night. Then as now, these stories also serve a cultural purpose; they convey crucial Crow ethics, values, and beliefs. From these stories Crow children learn what is expected from them in life and how they might achieve their desires. Therefore, these narratives also are a very important socializing tool.

Indeed, among the Crow the practice of storytelling is actually credited to the stars. The telling of stories is limited to the winter months because Old Woman's Grandson, the offspring of a human and the Sun, is said to have told the Crow that he wanted to hear his stories when he was around. Known as *Ihkaléaxe* or the "Bright Star" (Sirius), Old Woman's Grandson is visible throughout the winter nights, so his stories, as well as stories of other supernatural beings, are told in the winter.

Another commonly heard reason for this timing of storytelling is credited to the stars in general. The stars that have names, "the stars we know—*ihké aléwahkuua*," as elders often expressed it, are only visible at night; therefore, stories should be told when these stars that are known can be seen.

A complete description and analysis of the Crow oral performance style is beyond the scope of this work. However, some basic characteristics will provide insight into this style of oral tradition. Even when telling the stories in English, these attributes are apparent.

When relating events not actually witnessed by the teller, Crow people use the term *huuk*, which means, "they say." Also, for emphasis, words are lengthened. For example, the term for a distance away from the character is *ii*; when it is a great distance, the sound is lengthened, *iiii*. In English, storytellers will also lengthen terms for emphasis, such as, "It was waaay over there."

Storytellers also use repetition to clarify action, such as in the story of Old Woman's Grandson as told by the elder Carl: "So, she goes up there and the porcupine just goes higher and higher. She follows, but it just keeps going higher and higher." In the same story, when describing the habits of the Sun, the use of another technique, that of contrast, can be seen: "The Sun would leave at daybreak and be gone all day. Night, he would come back, day he would be gone." These examples of the performance style of Crow oral literature can be found in most if not all of the stories included in this book.

Another variance of Crow storytellers when relating the stories in English is the use of Crow words to stress statements or explain Crow philosophy, or when the storyteller simply does not know the English word. The former can be seen in the description of the cycle of the night as provided by Lloyd: ". . . they say that sounds are very audible from distances. They call it *bilikkukkuliixiassak* [voices are heard clearly]." The latter can be seen in the second story of the Woman Star as told by Nathan: "She went across three big rivers, put down her *bachipe* [digging stick] and crossed." When storytellers utilized Crow for any reason, it was preserved in the text with a literal translation in brackets, as in the examples above. Crow words were retained in translated pieces when the term was a proper noun or had no adequate English equivalent.

A general characteristic of Crow oral tradition is its malleability—stories differ from storyteller to storyteller. Often this is because of the storyteller's own kin or family tradition, which stressed specific parts of stories; or it may be because of the historic band group or present-day district origins of the individual narrator. It appears that some versions of stories are particular to specific communities on the reservation, whereas other stories vary within the same community. These variations for Crows are not problematic, they are simply recognized as differences. For example,

Inez, an elder from the Lodge Grass District, stated before beginning her version of the Big Dipper story:

> This one about the Seven Stars [Big Dipper] must be the one that is called Pipe Pointer Stars. I will tell you what I know about the Big Dipper. There will be others who will tell this story each in their own way. This is my version of the way I heard it.

In fact most storytellers open a storytelling session with a preamble that describes the lineage of the story, thus placing it in the context of a specific family and band/district group. A typical preamble of this sort was provided by Albert, an elder from Wyola:

> I listened to elders talk of things and I learned from them. There are many that I have learned from. There is one called Old Mouse, he was always telling stories. He loved to tell stories. This was his favorite pastime. Old Mouse was related to Yellow Brow. Yellow Brow was also a great storyteller. He knew much, he wouldn't miss anything, songs and various stories. Then there was Arms Around The Neck, he was a great one too. He was a chief. He lived with us until he died. I learned much from that old man. I have learned much from stories of our elder men.

In total twenty elders were interviewed for this project and sixteen described the use and importance of celestial phenomena. In some cases many elders knew the names of stars or constellations, but perhaps only one or two could describe the beliefs or practices associated with it. To provide clarity for the reader, and maintain privacy for these elders, pseudonyms have been provided. The pseudonyms were provided in alphabetical order to correspond to the chart (see opposite page) of the elders' stories.

Also, it should be noted that the Crow term *ihké* refers to a single star or a series of stars comprising a constellation. For this reason, when translating Crow names for constellations into English, it appears as star and not constellation. The only other term used to designate a constellation is the term *báakkaa*, which means "above."

Lastly, as with most aspects of the natural world, the Crow people have an intimate relationship with and respect for the stars, and they have strict and formal ways of interacting with them. It is considered inappropriate to point to the stars with the finger. Instead, a pointer, often a willow shoot, is used. The only time the moon and sun are pointed to is when making a vow or taking an oath. To address or greet the stars one simply extends the open hands.

The Crow people have developed a complex method of transferring their cultural knowledge and, in part, this knowledge has come from the stars. They have also tied their values and behaviors as well as their daily existence and very origins to the stars.

Stars and Constellations Described by Crow Elders																
Crow Star Name	**First Initial of Elder's Pseudonym**															
	A	B	C	D	E	F	G	H	I	J	K	L	M	N	O	P
Seven Brothers	X	X	X	X	X	X	X	X	X	X	X	X	X	X	X	X
Bright Star	X	X	X	X		X	X		X	X	X	X		X		X
Star That Does Not Move	X	X	X	X		X	X		X	X	X					
Day Star	X			X		X	X	X	X	X	X					
Star With A Tail	X	X	X	X		X		X							X	
Seven Bulls	X				X		X			X	X				X	
Hand Star	X	X				X						X				X
Where They Take Women		X	X		X			X	X							
Gathering Of Stars	X				X		X	X		X						
Bear Above	X			X	X								X			
Crazy Star	X		X		X											
Woman Star		X						X						X		
Campsite Star			X		X								X			
Weasel Star		X				X										
Goose Above		X	X													
Turtle Above				X				X								
Cougar Star				X	X											

Chapter 2

THE CROW PEOPLE AND THE STARS

Through stories the Crow people describe the heavens as a plane that over-arcs the earth. In this realm the sun, moon, and stars dwell with the clouds and the birds. The Crow term for the sky, *awaxé*, is often translated by Crow elders as "atmosphere," or another solid world that exists above the earth. The beings who exist in the above world are sometimes described as living much like humans, yet retaining characteristics of their true form. In physical terms, the stars specifically are believed to be spherical in shape. When Hanna, an elder from the Big Horn District, defined the Crow term for stars, *ihké*, she explained:

> The stars are, my grandmother would call them eggs since the word *ihké* means both a star and an egg. *Ihké* does not really mean a chicken egg or a bird's egg, I think it is something of, it is a material thing that is shaped like that. Like in the word for nit, not a louse, but the nit, they call it *bihké*, and it sounds like *ihké*, so it's the shape of a thing that we call *ihké*. So those are substances that are proportioned in that shape.

In spiritual terms, however, the stars are perceived as powerful beings who can provide assistance to humans. The Crow say that at the time of creation the Creator, *Iichíhkbaalee*, placed sacred power into all things. This is the power which the Crow term *baaxpée*. All things of creation, including the stars, are therefore sacred, and humans must rely on them to survive. Hanna commented:

> They look at the stars as beings. They feel that stars have power. I mean, they have power, being all the way out there, above, they have power. I have heard of people that have had certain stars as their help-ers. I know of one man whose medicine is the *Ihkaxaxuakáate* [the precious Gathering of Stars/Pleiades], or the Little Cluster of Stars, and I have heard them say that his medicine is this Little Group of Stars and so he always connects himself with that and he knows about them. That's his medicine and these stars are significant to him.

The stars, therefore, are seen as a very important group of potential supernatural patrons. Stars and other celestial phenomena are sought for the powers known to be possessed by those specific beings. Most stars and constellations that have been named, and that are attributed with certain powers or specific origins and his-tories, are collectively called *ihké aléwahkuua*—"the stars we know." Nonetheless, these stars are no more important than stars that are not named, for as elders often say, "All stars are sacred." In fact, it was from all the stars that the Crow received their Sacred Tobacco, the religious item which united and defined them as a nation.

CROW ORIGINS AND THE STARS

Crow oral tradition links the origin of the tribe to a separation from a parent group. Tradition relates that this group traveled extensively across the upper Midwest of the United States, and possibly into southern Canada. Eventually this parent group came under the lead-ership of two brothers known as No Intestines and Red Scout. These leaders had their respective followers and, even though they camped as one group, the two divisions were clearly defined within a single village. The group following No Intestines called themselves *Bíiluuke*, "Our Side," and they would become the historic Crow who eventually settled in Montana and Wyoming. The group under Red Scout would move to the Heart River area of North Dakota. They would learn hor-ticultural ways from the Mandan of that region and would become the historic Hidatsa tribe.

In addition, Crow oral tradition lends religious validity to this separation of the Crow and Hidatsa. Their narratives relate how the two leaders had fasted at Devil's Lake and each had received a vision. No Intestines received a vision which told him to seek the seeds of Sacred Tobacco, *Ihchichiaee*. After locating this tobacco, he and his followers would be in the center of the world—the best place for his people. Red Scout, on the other hand, received a vision instructing him to settle with his people on the bluffs above the rivers, and to plant corn on the floodplains below.

After the initial vision, No Intestines and his followers began a long trek west. Eventually, the *Biiluuke* stopped near Chief Mountain, in present-day Montana, and there No Intestines fasted again. On the fourth day he received a second vision telling him he was not yet at his destination, the area was too cold. Then the *Biiluuke* moved south, passing by Salt Lake, Utah. After awhile, No Intestines and his group reached the Canadian River in Oklahoma, called Arrowhead River by the Crow. Here, No Intestines fasted again and was told to move north. So the *Biiluuke* headed north, following the Missouri to the Platte River, then trekking to the Powder River which they followed north until they reached the Big Horn Mountains in northern Wyoming.

To the Crow the highest peak on the crest of the Big Horn Mountains is called *Awaxaawakússawishe*, "Extended Mountain," and it is considered the center of their world. On this peak No Intestines fasted for the fourth time and received a vision telling him that he

Awaxaawakússawishe, "Extended Mountain," in the Big Horn Mountains, Wyoming (photo by Peter Nabokov).

was in the right place, that the tobacco seed could be found at the bottom of *Awaxaaawakússawishe*. As he looked to the base of the mountain, he saw the seeds as "twinkling stars," *ihkaxáaxaaheetak*. The *Bíiluuke* then made their home in Montana and Wyoming, with the Big Horn Mountains as their heartland.

This initial locating and the subsequent planting of the tobacco seeds became the genesis of the Crow's Tobacco Society. Historically, the Tobacco Society was the central set of ceremonies and rituals of the Crow people. It is important to note that No Intestines saw the seeds of the Crow's Sacred Tobacco as stars and that those seeds were also perceived not only as a gift from the stars, but as stars themselves.

Over time the Tobacco Society became divided into a number of different chapters, one chapter being known as *Ihkammishé*, "The Stars." When members of this chapter dance at any of the official Tobacco Society gatherings, they carry slender shoots of willow, since this is what should be used to point at the stars or the tobacco. Throughout the dance they ritually gesture with the willow shoots, as if they were pointing at the stars and the growing tobacco plants. In this way they promote growth and prosperity for all Crow people.

Aside from the Tobacco Society, there are three other contemporary public rituals that utilize stars. These are the Native American Church, the Shoshone-Crow Sun Dance, and the sweatlodge.

Women of the Star Chapter of the Tobacco Society dancing at a Tobacco Society adoption. Pencil drawing by Max Big Man, 1926 (courtesy of the Museum of the Rockies, previously published in Davis, 1979).

CYCLE OF THE NIGHT

To understand the importance of the stars and constellations to the Crow people, it is important to know how they view the cycle of the night. Lloyd, an elder from Crow Agency, provided this "sequence of the night" as viewed by Crow people. He began by saying, "I'll tell you how the night goes."

> The nighttime and how we see the stars, and what it means to us. Being a part of the natural world, we are very observant of the things that are about, the heavenly bodies, the cycle of day and night, all these things. So we have some descriptions pertaining to the night.

> At the end of the day, the time when the sun is setting, just as the sun is setting, right about that time of sunset, it is observed with optimism. It tells us what kind of day the next day is going to be. If it is very bright and colorful and orange, just a beautiful sunset, it means it's going to be a good day the next day. So it makes us feel good to see this kind of sunset.

> Then shortly after the sun goes down it's *áhpee* [evening, sunset but still light] and the Evening Star appears. When the Evening Star, *Baappaaihké* [Day Star] appears, then they say that at that moment, at dusk, when things are still visible but not too clear, they say silhouettes of any objects are larger in appearance. It's sort of an optical illusion, but they say that objects appear larger than they actually are, they appear larger at that moment. Right after this dusk the full darkness comes on, *áhpaakaashe* [real evening] and the time of the dusk is past, they say that sounds are very audible from distances. They call it *bilikkukkulíixiassak* [voices are heard clearly]. That's how they describe it, people talking from a distance away, their conversation can be heard but they can't make out what is said. Sounds are very keen at that moment.

> Right about midnight time, close to midnight, around eleven or so, according to today's version of a clock. About that time they say *kanmilaxxapík* [now people are lying down], means that people have gone to bed now and they desire good dreams before they go to bed, and throughout the night everything's quiet. Then they observe, if it's a clear night, when they say *ihkaxáaxaaheetak* [the stars are sparkling] it means all the stars are brightly observed, the brilliance of the stars. They say it is a good time. Everything is quiet: no inclement weather or anything, and they observe that with good feeling, *ihkaxáaxaaheetak*. Then comes the middle of the night, midnight, *óotchiakuahiia* [middle of the night].

> Then toward the morning, going into morning hours, we call it, *kaláashik* [late night]. See, throughout that time everything is quiet.

Here, just before the Morning Star appears, it's *áashiisaak* [towards dawn]. This is *iisanchihpashé*, that means that's when it's darkest, *iisanchihpashé* [dark face]. Just before dawn that's when that happens, shortly afterwards the Morning Star appears, *Ihkaléaxe* [Bright Star], Sirius star.

When *Ihkaléaxe* appears they say that's one of the most sacred times throughout the night because they greet the Morning Star with good feeling. They say *Iichíhkbaalee* [First Maker] is closest right at that moment. That's how they describe that moment. Throughout the night, like I said, they desire good dreams. One of the philosophies behind this feeling is that *Iichíhkbaalee* will have communications with us through dreams. And they express and interpret good dreams and they want to share those good dreams with their immediate loved ones, immediate family, children, grandchildren, wife, grandparents, immediate family and others of their concerns.

Shortly after that comes *áashe* [dawn], then you hear the noises of the birds, birds are waking up. They're coming back into happiness again, happy times. One of the practices behind it is that we wake up with the birds and sing with them and rejoice with them right at that time. It means roll out early.

And then when the Old Man appears again, the sun, they call him *Isáahkaxaalia*, the Old Man. When he appears, we greet the day with optimism and appreciation, once again. We are coming into a new day. Then we ask for good things during that day. That's what it means. So the cycle of night, and how the stars play into it is very important because we observe the good things all about us.

It is obvious that Crow people are astute observers of the night sky, even constructing a time marker—a clock—from the appearance and physical characteristics of stars in the night sky. The nightly cycle is a small replica of what can be seen throughout the year.

STARS OF THE SEASONS

Historically the stars were used to provide a gauge to govern when families should gather as sub-bands, and from bands to tribe; or the reverse, when gatherings should disperse before the depletion of resources. Generally the Crow observe the stars during two time periods of the night: from sundown until about midnight and an hour or so before sunrise. As noted previously, the two terms applied to these time periods are *áhpaakaashe*, or "real evening," and *iisanchihpashé*, or "dark face." A few knowledgeable Crows watch the procession of stars throughout the night at any time of the year to glean information. However, most commonly, the stars that are considered predictors of the seasons are watched from sundown until an individual goes to sleep.

The star most often utilized as an indicator of the seasons is the Bright Star, or Sirius. Old Woman's Grandson told the Crow that he was afraid of newborn buffalo calves, so he would not appear when buffalo were calving, an event of the spring. Thus the disappearance of Sirius from the night sky indicates to Crows that spring is near, that buffalo will soon be having their young. This would signal the shift from winter seclusion to a gathering of sub-bands in terrain suitable for root collection.

Other stars and constellations which told the Crow what time of the year it was included the Crow constellations of Hand Star, Goose Above, Bear Above, and Old Campsite Star. The Goose Above, or Cygnus, alerted everyone when late fall had arrived. The Hand Star, a portion of Orion, indicated the beginning and end of winter. The Bear Above, Hercules, heralded the approach of spring, and the position of the Campsite Star, Corona Borealis, indicated the progress of summer. Another Crow constellation called the Weasel Star, a compilation of the bright stars of Draco, Cepheus, Cassiopeia, and Perseus, could be used throughout the year since it was circumpolar. Ben, an elder from the Pryor District, detailed how some of these constellations were utilized:

A constellation that is prominent in the stars is the Hand Star. It is usually in the east. The Crows used to look at that constellation. It is most prominent in the evening or early morning, so they looked at that star and when the hand was tilted to the left then they say that the birds will be coming soon. But in the evening the hand is straight up. Then, they will say that the birds will be leaving. So that's what they used the Hand Star for.

The Hand Star is the lower half of Orion. To the Greeks, Orion looked like a man. But when the Crows saw it, it was actually a left hand with all the fingers stretched out. So that's what it looked like to the Crows and that's what they called it, they called it *Ihkawaléische* [Hand Star].

Another star is what they call *Báakkaawiilee* [Goose Above], the Goose. The Northern Cross to the Crows looks like a goose. I think it is Cygnus. I'm sure that the Greeks called it Cygnus, but it's the Northern Cross, that's what they call it, and it looks like a cross and it's in the south. Look at the south and it looks like a cross.

But to the Crows it looks like a goose that's flying with the wings spread out. That's what they call it, *Báakkaawiilee*. The geese usually fly to the south in the fall, so that's why they call it the Goose Above. I guess they looked to the south when the geese were flying, were migrating, and they saw the cross and they said, "There is another goose all by itself, flying in the constellations." That is easy to spot and that's always in the south. I'm sure it is called Cygnus.

Albert, an elder from the Wyola area, described how the winter constellation of the Hand Star, the bottom half of the Euro-American constellation Orion, was utilized:

> This one that is called the Hand Star, at times really is bright. This Hand Star is an offering to the people of the earth, that is its meaning. The hand belonged to a being in the heavens. It was cut off and is still there. The people watch this star. In the winter this star is watched, studied, as is the moon. People watch both the moon and the Hand Star to predict the weather. At times it lights up so bright it stands out. At other times it is hard to spot. If it is easy to see then the next day will be clear, if it is hard to see then there will be weather. They watch this star throughout the winter. From the movement of the Hand Star people can tell the progress of winter. It is used for this purpose also.

The use of the stars to demarcate when gatherings should occur is reflected in the following description by Carl of the Old Campsite Star:

> *Annáshe* means a campsite, when you say *annáshe*, that could mean any campsite, but that particular constellation, that particular configuration looks like a circle. A circle of camps, or even like a tipi ring. *Ihkaannáshe* [Corona Borealis], the stars that are like the campsite, that is why they say *ihkaannáshe*. At Crow Fair time it is directly overhead.

The constellation known as *Báakkaalaxpitchee*, Bear Above, is used by the Crow to tell when early spring has arrived. Bear Above is part of the Euro-American constellation known as Hercules. The bear is a significant animal to the Crow. He is addressed as "brother" and is seen as the one who controls the mountains on the reservation. The bear is admired for its strength, bravery, and courage. The bear is also seen as protective of his home or area. These qualities are remembered whenever the Bear Above constellation is seen.

This constellation can be viewed in early spring and is visible until the fall. In the past the appearance of Bear Above marked the time when eagle trapping began. The most desired feathers were from the tails of immature golden eagles, and the Crow say that young golden eagles have the desired plumage when Bear Above is first visible in spring. This relationship is reinforced by the tradition that it was the bear that taught the Crow how to trap eagles. Carl also correlated the relationship to an explanation for the spring thunderstorms:

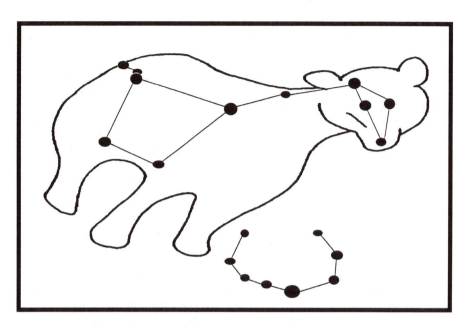

Bear Above (Hercules) and Old Campsite Star (Corona Borealis).

When Bear Above appears in the spring is when young eagles are losing their downy feathers. The bear is the enemy of the eagle, so when Bear Above appears in the spring, the Thunderbird, who is a bald eagle, becomes disturbed. This is why there are tremendous thunderstorms in the spring and early summer.

The importance of this constellation is also underscored by a popular story about how Bear Above adopted a little boy named White Bear Cub. It is believed that the two main characters of this narrative are historical figures. The tyrannical One Eye is often described as not just a clan leader, but the leader of the whole Crow Tribe. Although White Bear Cub became a powerful shaman as an adult, in this story he is a poor orphan boy. Matthew, an elder from the Two Leggings area, provided this version:

In distant times Crow clans would fight each other. One time the Piegan Clan and the Whistling Water Clan were fighting. The leader of the Piegan Clan was named One Eye, he was powerful. He would take the property and the wives of Whistling Water clan members. They were afraid of his power.

One day the camp moved towards a buffalo herd. As the camp moved, they came to a creek. When the group stopped for water, One Eye noticed an orphan boy named *Daxpitcheeláakchiash* [White Bear Cub]. One Eye went up to where White Bear Cub was bent over, drinking water, and stepped on his neck, which forced his head under the water and caused him to drown. This boy had no parents and was a member of the Whistling Water clan. He was well liked by the members of that clan.

When the camp moved off, White Bear Cub regained consciousness, but instead of returning to the group, he went to the mountains. In the mountains he fasted and cried. A bird came to him and told him that Bear Above was going to adopt him in the spring. The boy spent the winter in the mountains. That spring Bear Above came to him in the form of a man. He told the boy that he had adopted One Eye but didn't like the way he was acting and how he was treating his tribesmen. He told White Bear Cub that he would adopt him and gave him a piece of bear sinew. He told the boy that when he returned to camp to not fear One Eye, and to throw the sinew in the fire and One Eye would die.

The boy returned to the camp. The Whistling Waters were overjoyed to see him alive. One Eye pretended to also be glad to see the boy, but he feared that the boy had been adopted by a strong being or else he would not be back. White Bear Cub was now a young man and he thought he would take one of One Eye's wives to insult him. He went to a young wife of One Eye and told her to come with him. She was afraid, but White Bear Cub told her he was adopted by One Eye's father, so she agreed.

When One Eye found out he sent presents and word that the marriage was okay with him. White Bear Cub went anyway and threw the sinew in the fire. One Eye doubled over as the sinew burned and he died. White Bear Cub threw in all the sinew and said he did that because he never wanted to use his power against his own people again.

Retribution against those who have wronged others may not be possible at the immediate moment. However, this story teaches that the Powers, including the stars, will help those who have been persecuted.

CIRCUMPOLAR STARS

There are two Crow constellations that are circumpolar, that is, they are visible throughout the year. They are the Weasel Star and the Seven Stars, or Big Dipper. The Big Dipper serves two purposes outside of its importance to Crow religious philosophy: first as an aid to locate the North Star or Polaris for directional orientation, and second as a way to calculate the passing of time. Various elders have described how both purposes served Crow war parties that were traveling at night. Probably this is how the Big Dipper became associated with the Crow concept that these seven stars were seven brothers who were led by a war party leader, and the concept that it brought war parties together.

Ben, an individual from Pryor, described this crucial guiding function of the Big Dipper as follows:

> I want to talk about the North Star or Polaris. We call that *Ihkaxachíis-see*. A literal translation is, the star that does not move around. Polaris is in the north. You can usually tell it by the Big Dipper. If you can find the Big Dipper and then, find the end opposite of the handle, then you look straight from the two stars from the opposite of the handle, then you will see Polaris. That's how I was told when I was a little boy, so I've always found Polaris by looking at the Big Dipper.
>
> The Crows used the stars to find direction and to know where they were when it was night, during the night. For instance, when I was younger and I used to work on ranches or when I used to be out riding, I used to look for the Big Dipper all the time so I would know

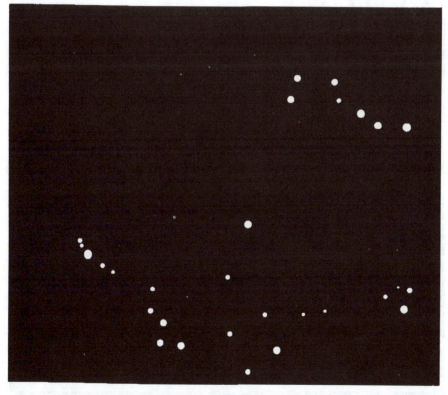

The two circumpolar constellations of the Crow. Top, the Seven Stars (Big Dipper); bottom, the Weasel Star (Draco, Cepheus, Cassiopeia, and Perseus); and center, the Star That Does Not Move (Polaris).

exactly where I was at. Sometimes I would be working at a place I had never been before, and I always used the *Ihkaxachíissee* or Polaris to get my direction and my bearing.

As a way to calculate the passage of time at night, many Crows who have and use this knowledge today are the Native American Church leaders who are called Road Men or Road Chiefs. Their night-long ceremonies are coordinated with the movement of the Big Dipper through the night sky, as it marks when certain aspects of the ceremony should take place. Although most Road Men today use

A Crow Road Man praying at midnight. The Seven Stars and the Star That Does Not Move appear in the upper right. This illustration is a reproduction of a scene painted on a Crow Native American Church kit box. Pine box painted with watercolors, artist unknown, 1980s (author's collection, line drawing by author).

wristwatches to keep track of the progress of the ceremony, a number of Road Men still employ the Big Dipper as their ritual clock.

When I showed one Road Man a sheet I had developed of Crow stars and constellations (see frontispiece), he immediately said, "It's early evening, about 7:00, 7:30," for he saw the right edge of the sheet as the horizon and as such the position of the Big Dipper in the drawing indicated early evening in mid-fall, the time of the year I showed him my drawing. Another Road Man added, "When the Big Dipper somersaults, it's going to be morning. When the bowl is over here it is the evening [indicating east of Polaris] and when it's here [indicating west of Polaris] it's morning." This observation was echoed by yet another Peyotist who said, "When the Big Dipper turns completely around the North Star, morning is not far behind." By observing the position of the Big Dipper at dusk, the Road Men are able to calculate the passage of time throughout the night.

Hanna, an elder from the Big Horn District, commented on the position of the Big Dipper during the "dark face time" each month, since this is when she prays and she therefore can regulate the passage of the months:

> With the Seven Stars, the Big Dipper, they could tell time. At the beginning of each month the tail is in a different position, like in the fall months, where the tail is at what time of the evening or of morning, or whatever. I remember at the beginning of last October, when I went out at the dark face time, about four o'clock in the morning, I went out there and looked and the tail was straight down. And so that's the way they kind of told time from month to month.

The other circumpolar Crow constellation, the Weasel Star, is actually composed of four Euro-American constellations: part of Draco makes the head, Cepheus the front legs and chest, Cassiopeia the hind end and back legs, and part of Perseus makes the tail. This constellation can be seen at any time of the year since it is circumpolar, so the position of the Weasel Star against the background of stars and the horizon line provides a rough indication of the time of year. Ben, an elder from the Pryor District, elaborated on this important constellation:

> When the Crows looked at the constellations, they saw a weasel. They used the weasel also to tell summer from winter. It's most prominent in the evening and in the morning. The weasel is a combination of Draco. Standing here at Pryor, Draco is usually to the north, direct north. The head of the weasel is Draco, and it looks like a weasel's head. There are three prominent stars and it's pointed like a weasel's head. And then coming down is part of Cepheus. Cepheus is the two arms. Then there are some other stars that are a combination of this

and it looks like a weasel's body. And also Cassiopeia is the lower half of the weasel, so it takes most of the northern part of the night sky.

In the summer it looks like it is lying down, it's on its back, but in the wintertime they say it is standing up and it is growling. *Kammáalaachicheek Uuttee, ihkaúuttee kan iluuák ihaashík, heelichiiluuk* ["Now it looks like winter. Weasel, the Weasel Star is standing and growling." That's what they say]. That is how they tell it is wintertime and they say it's going to be cold. *Iluuák ihaashík, heelichiiluuk* ["He's standing and growling," they say]. So that's the start of wintertime like in December or January. And in the summer it's almost lying down on its back, so it's summertime. So that's one of the ways that they can tell, they say it is going to be cold or hot. It's going to be extremely hot because the weasel is lying down.

That is part of Draco, Cepheus, and Cassiopeia. I think it is part of Perseus also. The tail is really distinctive, almost like the outlines of Perseus. That's one of the constellations. It is easy to tell because it actually looks like a weasel. Look for the head, Draco, and it's easy to tell. It is the most prominent in the early evening and also in the early morning like two, three o'clock. That is one of the ways to get your bearing at night. If you can see the weasel, you are looking at the north.

More than directions can be gleaned from star watching. Fay, an elder from the Black Lodge District, gave a description of how her father used the Weasel Star to determine the weather:

My father used to go out at night and check the stars. He would wait for a certain time. He'd go out and stay out for a long time. During the night he'd stand outside and look north, south, east, and west. He would stand to the four winds, not moving, and then he would pray, to see what the next season would be. He wanted to know what the weather was going to be like in the coming season.

Like if it is the fall he'd get out there and look at the stars. He would look this way, then that way—to the four winds. He said that the stars would move and change their positions, except for one star, it is the North Star. It doesn't ever move to another place, but remains at one place. "The Star That Doesn't Move," they call it. It never moves, it just stays there all the time.

Around this star is one star [constellation] called the Weasel Star. It looks like a weasel and it moves around the North Star. My father said that he always would watch this star. As winter is coming, he would go outside and listen. He wanted to know what the winter would be like. He would go outside and listen. This weasel is a spirit or something holy and it would tell him what was going to happen.

Then he would come in after he had received the message. He would not tell us until the next morning. He would say, "It is going to be a hard winter, I hear the Weasel roaring." He would ask us to get a lot of firewood, for we would need it, for the hard winter that was coming. The next year, he would go through the same thing. "The winter is going to be a short winter this year," he'd say, "We're going to be all right, it is good. The heavy part of winter is going north of us into Canada, or, maybe the blizzard weather will go way down in Wyoming. It will not come our way. Even though the snow may cover the grass, the top of the grass shows through. There will be food for our horses."

He knows by the stars. He would always be watchful of the stars. It was a medicine man that told him about that. One night this medicine man went outside with my father and showed him and gave him the story behind it.

Stars are an integral part of the Crow understanding of time, whether it is short term—as in nights or seasons—or long term—as in a year. Their thorough knowledge of stars and their movements allows them to prepare for the next moment or season, even today.

Chapter 3

THE BRIGHT STAR

STARS OF THE MORNING

Among the Crow the Morning Star is referred to as *Ihkaléaxe*, or the "Bright Star." Although this term applies to any star that is brighter than usual which appears before sunrise, it specifically applies to Sirius, the most brilliant of the stars in the northern skies. Crow people say that their stories are told in the winter because the Morning Star wants to hear his story, and in the wintertime he is visible all night.

All versions of the Morning Star story end with a human personification of the Morning Star, the being known as Old Woman's Grandson, stating that he will not come when buffalo are having their young. Only after they are born will he appear as the Morning Star. And this timing corresponds to the known cycle of Sirius. For it appears as a night star all winter until late spring and early summer when it is no longer visible. In late July it shows itself briefly again, just before the sun rises, and then it appears for longer and longer periods until it is visible all night once again. Therefore, it is not visible during the time when buffalo are giving birth, late May to early July. The Morning Star, whether Sirius or any of the other

stars or planets, is important not only because it heralds the beginning of the day, but also because it marks the end of *iisanchihpashé*, the "dark face time"—the holiest time of the night.

One of the ways by which Crow people seek to communicate
with the supernatural world is through fasting, the practice known
as *bilisshíissannee*, or "not drinking water." When Crow people fast
they seek a secluded area alone, often in the mountains. There they
go without water and food for as much as four days. This is done in
hopes of obtaining the favor of a supernatural patron, a being who
will provide them with holy power so that they may gain the things
they desire. The Crow believe that the strongest communications
with the supernatural occur through dreams or visions which take
place during the "dark face time." And some attribute visions in general to the Morning Star, *Ihkaléaxe*.

Another expression of spirituality among the Crow is the Native
American Church or Peyote Way. This indigenous religion is char-
acterized by night-long meetings which include singing and prayer
along with the sacramental consumption of the spineless cactus,
peyote. This form of worship originated in Mexico in pre-Columbian
times and spread to southern Plains Indians, Kiowas, Comanches,
and Cheyennes through Mescalero Apache intermediaries in the
mid-1800s.

The Crow adopted the Peyote Way from their Northern Cheyenne
neighbors in 1890. They have since integrated it with their beliefs
and practices, often utilizing clan fathers and clan mothers to serve
as officers—Road Man, Drum Man, Fire Man, and Water Woman—in
the meetings. Crow star knowledge has also been incorporated into
this important expression of spirituality. Carl, an elder from the Big
Horn District, related how the Crow philosophy of the Morning Star
and the "dark face time" is used in the Native American Church
practice of having a woman bring water and offer a prayer as a con-
clusion to the night-long meeting:

> This Native American Church is not original Crow; it came from the
> south. But in many ways it fits what we know about the Crow way, and
> we put the two together. They say there's a time of the night no matter
> where you are, where just before the Morning Star comes, the moon
> has set, if there is a moon, and the stars are not as lustrous as other
> times, and it's really really dark. So that is when the Morning Star
> comes. It seems like a new light, the morning, the dawn.
>
> So somewhere in the moments before the Morning Star comes into
> view, they say that's the darkest of the night. They call it dark face,
> *iisanchihpashé*. That means that even though you're familiar with
> somebody and you meet them, you have to really look; it is so dark the
> commonness does not come through.

They say at that moment the First Maker gets real close to the ground and listens so that when you make a pleading He'll hear you. So, when you want to, when you want to be very profound, and you want to extend maximum effort in offering a prayer, that is the time to say it.

So, that's why we use cedar, offer smoke, and have a woman offer prayer, because there's no prayer as sincere and as full of love as a mother's prayer for her child. So when she offers prayer for her child and includes us, then First Maker will hear it through the best channel.

In this manner, Crow people make a metaphoric link between the love of a mother for her children and Creator's love for all people. Kirk, another elder, echoed Carl's statement when he explained the progress of a Native American Church meeting:

When it's morning, like somewhere between three-thirty, four o'clock in the springtime or summertime, about that time the Morning Star is usually out and they say the Creator is pretty close to Mother Earth—when darkness turns into daylight. This is considered the most sacred time of the day. The Road Man sings his morning water song and the woman brings in water and prays.

Of course, dawn prayers are important outside of the Native American Church context, too. Hanna, a woman from the Big Horn District, discussed how she learned about the "dark face time" and how she carries on the practice of the pre-dawn prayer:

The *iisanchihpashé*, "dark face time," is right early in the morning, just before the sun rises, just before dawn it is the darkest, *iisanchihpashé*, and everything seems to be darker than night at that time. Then suddenly it's the day, it's bright.

This "dark face time" though is very dark, it is just like you're standing out there and all at once it is just a film of darkness over you. It is extremely dark, it's an eerie time, it really is, it's an eerie time. You wonder why that happens, what kind of a belt went over the earth.

Then you notice the plants, the trees around, they start to move a little bit, when it starts to subside, they move a little bit, just like they know the sun is coming up and as soon as it clears it seems like they kind of settle down. That is what I've observed up there where I'm at, they do move, they do move just like they're waking up or something and when the sun clears the sky, they settle right back down.

Now this time, this "dark face time" was the time when my grandmother would pray, during that time she would go out and pray and I would watch for her because I was afraid something might happen to her in the dark. But I could see her silhouette so I would come back and wait in the robes, in the buffalo robes. I use to love to sleep with her in the buffalo robes. I slept with my grandmother on the floor in old buffalo robes when I was a child and I still do, I like to go back to the buffalo robe, it's so nice I feel contented in there.

Well, she use to wait until it began to burst light, that darkness lifted. The light that comes between the dark face time and the rising of the sun they say *bilítaachiixaake*, they are saying the brightness of the moon, but it means morning, daylight, daybreak, a dawn type light. During this time she would come in and have a cold cup of coffee from the night before. She would sit there still talking low, whether in prayer, whether it's reminiscing, talking about something in the past or something that is now happening, something that's about to happen. After she drank that coffee, she would just go back to bed for awhile again and then when the sun rose she was up.

It was a routine of hers that she did until she couldn't anymore. I follow that, and do that still, because I'm accustomed to that I guess, since I grew up with her.

Through uncounted generations, Crow grandmothers have passed on traditional knowledge by practice and observation. Beyond its importance as an indicator of approaching daytime, the Morning Star is also considered a powerful patron who grants his powers unwillingly. Once they are given, however, the fortunate recipient will almost certainly become successful. Albert, an elder from Wyola, described the instructions he received from his grandfather concerning the Morning Star as a spiritual patron and also his grandfather's conflict with a Christian proselytizer:

As the one that appears before daybreak, it is a very important star. You are not to point to it. He overcame a lot of enemies to be where he is, so you should respect him and offer him great gifts. We are told on down through the generations, not to point at this star. The one that comes in the morning at daybreak is thought to be the most powerful one. He is the greatest one.

The Bright Stars, I am told, adopted our elders. The Bright Stars are sacred, I am told. I was given the medicine of my grandfather. The reason that I am saying this is that my grandfather said, "That Morning Star adopted me." This medicine and its song was given to me. My grandfather adopted another man, so he also sings that song. There are two of us that have that.

He said, "Don't point at that star. He is sacred." Baptists told him it is the Devil. We don't know for a fact, but they said that it is the Devil. Bird Far Away [a Baptist lay-minister at Lodge Grass in the 1920s] spoke to him about it. He told my grandfather that the Morning Star may have a lot of different stories about it, but it is the Devil. Maybe Baptists are afraid of this star [laughs].

I want to sing the song to this medicine [he sings the song]. What this song means is when they ask for something from the Morning Star, it turns out. They want it and they sing the song and it comes. This star adopted my grandfather and I have that medicine now.

Native people enter into personal relationships with celestial phenomena, as Albert's story illustrates. Debra from the Reno District described how the Morning Star could become a powerful patron for an aspiring warrior:

> That Morning Star turns itself into an eagle and then this star helps a person when they go out fasting. This star would turn into an eagle and then he would help him when he fights. I know of one man that this Morning Star helped. When this man was a warrior this star would come down as an eagle, it comes down they say. This one man, when he's in a battle that star comes as an eagle and gives him powers to fight.

The importance of the Morning Star in Crow cosmology is underscored by the diversity of artwork that incorporates its symbolic representations. The Morning Star can be represented by a cross or by four elongated triangles in painting, beadwork, and other forms of traditional media.

In the Crow Native American Church the significance of the Morning Star is also brought out through art. In their meetings it is evoked by the manner in which the hide of the drum is tied to the cast iron kettle that forms the drum's body. The seven-yard rope that fastens the leather drumhead to the kettle is laced in such a way as to produce a seven-pointed star on the bottom of the drum. Most

Front cover of the Morning Star hoop bundle of Bull Shows painted with a representation of the Morning Star, mid-1800s. The Crow, in common with other American Indian people, depict stars with four points rather than the Euro-American practice of five points (courtesy of the National Museum of the American Indian, Smithsonian Institution, catalog #12/3100, photo by Pam Dewey).

Crow elders say this "rope star" represents the Morning Star, but one said that it actually represents the entirety of stars in the night sky.

In addition, the Morning Star often appears on the narrow, wooden or leather boxes in which the personal ritual items of Native American Church members are stored—what are termed "kit boxes." These painted containers frequently depict the woman bringing the morning water, as described earlier, and the Morning Star is prominently displayed to indicate that it is dawn at the time of her arrival.

A Water Woman waiting to bring in the morning water at a Native American Church meeting. The Morning Star is represented in the upper right. This drawing is a reproduction of an illustration painted on a Crow Native American Church kit box. Pine box painted with watercolors, artist unknown, 1980s (author's collection, line drawing by author).

THE OLD WOMAN'S GRANDSON

Crow people tell about the origins of the Morning Star in their narratives of *Káalisbaapitua*, or "Old Woman's Grandson." The term *káalisbaapite* is used to designate an individual who was or is being raised by a grandmother, still a common practice among the Crow. The term is likewise applied to a child who does not obey his parents, just like the original *Káalisbaapitua*. The grandmother in this story is generally identified with the moon.

In the following version of this popular narrative, *Káalisbaapitua* raids Moon's garden and she, in turn, discovers it's a boy by leaving gender-related toys at the garden and seeing which ones were played with the next day. This method of identifying the sex of a child is utilized today by expectant Crow mothers at a spring near Pryor called *Baakáatitshiwishe*, "Where There Are Children's Footprints." This small pool of water is concealed by a sandstone overhang and surrounded by young cottonwoods and willows. At this place pregnant Crow women sometimes leave a bow and arrows, for a boy, and a doll and ball, for a girl, in the belief that whichever set of toys is played with in their absence reveals the sex of their unborn child. This version of the Old Woman's Grandson story was told by Carl from St. Xavier:

There is a young lady who's so desirable that everybody wants her, but she won't take anybody. She is a good woman, skilled at all the womanly crafts. She's very good at quill work, so she's always catching porcupines for their quills for her handiwork.

So she and her friend are out when they see this porcupine. They talk about it, "Well, we should get someone to get it for us," says the friend. "No, I'll get it," she replied. So, she took a stick, and she was going to pry it out of the tree, because once they're on the ground anybody can get them. So, she goes up there and the porcupine just goes higher and higher. She follows, but it just keeps going higher and higher. Pretty soon her friend says, "You're going too high, something's wrong, this is unusual, this is unnatural, come down." "No, I got to get this," she said. She just keeps going until finally she gets so high she is way out of this world. And she goes beyond a particular barrier, and she's in a different land.

A fine looking young man all dressed in buckskin, light colored buckskin, comes. He's the sun, Old Man Sun, "I sent for you. I want you for my wife." So they became happily involved as man and wife. And they have a son. For his boy to play with, the Sun made a set of arrows and a bow. When he gave the boy the bow and arrows, he said, "You must never shoot a meadowlark." To his wife he said, "You can have any-

The author (left) and Crow Astronomy Project consultant Grant Bulltail (right) at "Where There Are Children's Footprints," 1996 (photo by Doug Kuhlman).

thing you want, I have the power to do anything. We'll raise a fine son. But there's just one thing you must never do, you must never turn over the buffalo droppings."

She was out digging roots one day and the boy was playing, shooting his arrows at different things. A meadowlark came around, flying around the boy. The boy talked to the bird, "Leave me alone." But the meadowlark kept flying around the boy. The boy got mad and shot at the bird, but just missed it. The bird then scolded the boy, "You are not one of us, you are a human, go back to where you came from."

The boy cried and ran off. At this same time the mother, without think-ing, turned over a buffalo chip. There was a hole in the ground and she could see right down to where her people were camped. She recog-nized people, sites, and everything. Right then the boy ran up and she put it back, and they went back to their place.

The Sun would leave at daybreak and be gone all day. Night, he would come back, day he would be gone. He came back and he immediately told her, "You did what I told you not to do." She wouldn't acknowl-edge it, but he knew. She got more lonely, more lonely, more home-sick. Then he told her, "You violated my condition, now you can't stay here. You could've had all this, but no more. So I'll send you back. What I am going to do, I am going to kill a hundred buffalo, and you make sure that you save the sinew out of each one, whole, complete. Don't make it short, make it complete."

So he brought her the sinew from a hundred buffalo. She took the sinew out of each one, and being a craftsperson, she did a complete job on all of them. When she got done, he took her to where the opening was, where she had turned over the buffalo chip. He fashioned a seat for her and her little baby, and tied all those sinew together and let them down. "Go home now and you'll forget all about this," he said as he lowered them.

It turned out that she left out one sinew, so she could not quite reach the ground, and because of the condition being violated he couldn't bring them back. He goes through the agony of deciding what to do, "If I save my son, I'll have to destroy her."

He picks up a rock and throws it at his wife. He strikes her with the rock. It strikes her and kills her, knocking her to the ground, but the baby is okay. Now, the little guy doesn't have a mother, so he's literally lost. In his sleep a snake gets into his skull. Pretty soon the snakes multiply, and that's snakes on the brain [laughs]. He's going crazy until the father looks down and sees that this can't go on forever. So, to save his son, he literally kills him by making it so stormy and so wet that the boy drowns. His head is full of water.

Then he clears up the skies and makes it so hot that the boy literally bakes, and the steam drives out all the snakes. But in so doing he just empties his head. That's when they put little rocks in his head. When he shakes his head it rattles. They call him "Uses His Head Like A Rat-tle."

But now he's free to roam again with all this tremendous power that comes from his father, Sun. He needs to eat, so he searches around and finds a garden. He keeps raiding this garden. He takes things from the garden. The garden belongs to an old lady. She says, "Something's here stealing my things; it's either a boy or a girl. I'll find out." So, she put out dolls and a ball, little girl things. They were untouched, but part of her garden was gone. "Ah! I bet you it's a boy," so she left bows and arrows and hoops—boy stuff. Sure enough they were played with, her pumpkins were all shot with arrows. "Now I know how to get him," she says. So she cooks up the favorite food of little boys. So, when he comes, she lures him. And now he's got a place to stay.

Now, the old grandma's wise and she'd say, "There's something evil over here. Don't you go there now. Don't you go near that, it's dangerous." The little boy's curiosity gets the best of him and he goes, and as soon as he finds these things he destroys them.

All kinds of things with little tricks, like the killing tree. The killing tree was on a trail; people would come along, the tree would fall and kill them, and go back up. So he goes and pretends to go under the tree, but jumps back. He keeps doing that until he smashes it. Then there was a rock that rolls on people. He gets it to roll about until it smashes itself into little pieces. Then there's the old lady, the cannibal with a magic kettle. The kettle sucks people in and cooks them. The boy turns it on her and kills her. The water that devours people, same thing. And finally a sucking bull that sucks people in. The boy is sucked in but cuts his way out, freeing all those who were caught before him.

But in the process, the little man had never seen a newborn calf before. When he saw the calf, with its bulging eyes and its yellow hooves, he gets scared, runs up in a tree, stays there. He would almost perish there, until his father saves him again by bringing on weather which drives the calf away. So, when his work was done, he went to the heavens and became the Morning Star, *Ihkaléaxe*. But when it's calving time, he never comes back because he's still afraid of calves.

The stone which is said to have been thrown by the Sun to kill his human wife was known by Crow people to be located on the Ft. Berthold Reservation in North Dakota. When the Ft. Berthold Reservation was formed in the 1880s, a Hidatsa family moved the stone to their allotment and cared for it. Both the Hidatsa and the Crow continued to revere this stone until the 1950s, when Garrison Dam was built on the Missouri River and the back waters flooded the area where the stone was located. Before that time, the Hidatsa would paint the stone with sacred red ocher and leave gifts of yard goods. When visiting their sister tribe, Crows would often visit the stone, leaving money, tobacco, and other gifts out of respect for its importance in their cosmogony and cosmology.

An elder from the Black Lodge area recalled that as a boy he and his family visited the Hidatsa caretakers of this stone. While there, he spent his days ice skating on a nearby creek with their children. Before they left, to return home to Montana, he watched his father offer coins and pray at the stone.

Stone that killed Old Woman's Grandson's mother at the feet of Hidatsa care-taker James Holding Eagle, 1950 (courtesy of the State Historical Society of North Dakota, photo by George Metcalf).

When another elder from the St. Xavier District, Oscar, reiterated the importance of the stone, he contrasted the story of *Káalisbaapitua* to Christian beliefs:

> They say the Sun has a child on this earth. He is sacred. He is called *Káalisbaapitua*. This is as I know it. The white man's religion states that God has a son, but it is a little different from our *Káalisbaapitua*. According to our way of belief the First Maker has no children, but the Sun, the Old Man, he has a child. This happened while we were in the area of the Hidatsa.

The women used to get the porcupine quills and use them to decorate their things since there were no beads at that time. Once a beautiful woman went after a porcupine. The porcupine went higher and higher until it broke through the skies and came to a home. The Sun welcomed her and said, "It is good you have come." They married and had a child and the Sun told her don't pick wild turnips or turn over the buffalo chips. To his son he said, "Don't kill the meadowlark." But as boys are crazy, he threw something at the meadowlark.

The meadowlark mocked this boy, "This is not your home. Go home now." The father knew this thing that had happened. He killed a buffalo and got the sinews to make a rope to return his wife and boy to the earth, but he forgot one and it didn't reach the ground. The mother and child were hanging above the ground. The Sun picked up a stone and spoke to it, "It is not the child, it is the woman you must kill." He threw the stone and it killed the woman, the little boy was okay. Way over where the Hidatsas are at, where the dam is, the stone is located. It is there. It is a big stone. It is sacred. It is a part of our history.

When a people's history is intimately linked to an object of this earth, it is easy to understand why people fight so tenaciously to hold onto the object and the land on which it is located. Crow people are tied not only to tangible objects, like the Sun's stone, but also to ephemeral ones, like the stars. Being in contact with proper perspective on stone or sky gives Crow people a sense of rootedness, as well as examples of proper actions and sanctions for improper ones. The very earth and sky themselves are Crow textbooks.

Chapter 4

PLANETS
THE UNPREDICTABLE STARS

The Crow generally perceive planets as unpredictable stars. Their varying yearly cycles coupled with their general brightness of color or colors has made them of special interest. Oftentimes the brightest object at sunrise or sunset is a planet rather than a star. The brightest object that appears over the horizon shortly before sunrise is Morning Star, while that which appears with or just after sunset is Evening Star. While the Morning Star has been extensively addressed in the last chapter, it should be understood that the term *Ihkaléaxe*, "Bright Star," can apply to any brighter-than-usual heavenly body: Sirius, Venus, Mercury, Mars, Jupiter.

The Evening Star is similar; any brighter than usual star or planet appearing in the evening would be termed *Baappaaihké*, "Day Star," the general term used for an Evening Star. However, as the term implies, this is a star that is visible even in daylight. As the elder Ben, from Pryor, stated, "It is called the Evening Star, but it likes the day better, so we call it *Baappaaihké*, Day Star." This description suggests that the Crow are referring to Venus, which is bright enough to be seen even while the sun is still up. Inez, an elder from Lodge Grass, described this phenomenon:

43

In the evening just as the sun goes down, there is a star that comes out that is called *Baappaaihké* [Day Star], this is the Evening Star. It is the one that is referred to as the star that appears during the day.

Although there are no specific stories of the origin of this star, Crows desire it as a spiritual patron and it is seen as an indicator of when night officially begins. In this respect, its appearance is important for timing the beginning of religious ceremonies, such as meetings of the Native American Church, or the nighttime prayer meetings of the Sun Dance adherents, which are called "Full Moon Bundle Openings." This use of the Evening Star was explained by Hanna, an elder from the Big Horn District:

They say the Evening Star is kind of a first star, it is the first one of the night. It marks the beginning of the night. And sometimes it can be seen during the daytime, before dark or dusk.

Fay, an elder from the Black Lodge District, described her father's relationship with the Evening Star:

My father would pray to the Evening Star. He would say, "It is night now and I am blessed, that you have watched over us until now." He sent word up there. At night he would go outside and look up to the skies and he can see the Evening Star.

Venus, which is sometimes Morning Star and sometimes Evening Star, is also known as *Ihkawaaláaxe*, or the "Crazy Star," because of its erratic cycle coupled with its varying brightness and color: red, white, green, and blue. Carl, an elder from Big Horn District, stated:

I'll talk about the Crazy Star, *Ihkawaaláaxe*. From what I've heard and from observations, I would say it's Venus. They call it crazy because it is not consistent, changes color, flashes differently, sparkles differently, and it doesn't stay, and then it comes back, doesn't always come back in the same place, sometimes in the east, sometimes in the west. That's why they call it crazy, it's unpredictable. They didn't use it to fix seasons or times, as sometimes it is an Evening Star, sometimes it's the Morning Star. Because of that, it's called the Crazy Star. The Crazy Star is not sought for its religious power, since it is thought to give power easily but not steadily, because of its generally unpredictable nature.

Albert, an elder from Wyola, summarized the teachings he had received from his elders concerning the Bright Stars:

The Bright Star is very powerful, but I was told by my elders that there are four Bright Stars. The first one, the Evening Star, is in the west. If you see it just before it becomes dark, it will really be bright about that time, that's why it is called the Day Star. It is also called the Bright Star.

There is the one that appears before sunset in the west. If you see it at sunset it really sparkles [Venus/Day Star]. There is the one from the time the Evening Star shows up to the time that the Morning Star comes [Sirius].

After the moon goes down then there appears the next one, the Morning Star [Venus/Morning Star]. The fourth one is erratic, if you look at this one it does things like lights up real bright, then darkens up, it moves around then stops. It moves up, then down [Venus/Crazy Star].

THE WOMAN STAR

Mars is also well known to the Crow and it has two names, *Ihkaw-ilée*, "Fire Star," and *Ihkawía*, "Woman Star." The first name derives from its bright red color. The origin of the second name is described in two stories which feature a sinister character known as *Hisshish-tawia*, the "Very Red Woman." She is a complex character, sometimes identified as helping with the creation of the world, but more often seen as a treacherous, self-interested cannibal. Usually she carries a root-digging stick as her principal tool. The next two narratives, plus the one of the Twins that follows, emphasize her dangerous nature.

The *Awakkulé*, or "Little People," which appear in the first story, are small humanlike beings who are believed to inhabit mountainous, remote areas of the Crow Reservation. They are known to be both shy and mischievous. Generally helpful to the Crow, they still like to play tricks on unsuspecting humans. Since Pryor is close to one of their best-known haunts, the Little People are often associated with this community. This version of the Woman Star story was provided by Ben, an individual from Pryor, which may be why it has the benevolent Little People coming to the rescue of the main character:

> Early in the morning, I think it's Mars, there is a star that is prominent. They say it looks red. When they were telling me about this star they say you look at it and it looks red early in the morning. So I think it's Mars. They call that the "Woman Star" or *Ihkawía*.
>
> This star is a beautiful woman that would not marry anyone, young men who proposed to marry her were refused, until a man called *Iisbishéetbishe* [Worms In His Face] came along. When this man saw her, he put love magic on her. After this spell was put on her, he had control of her mind. This man lived towards the sunrise, beside a large stream. The young woman walked along until she came to his house. Eventually they were married.

At a point she came to realize this man was *Iisbishéetbishe*, and she wanted to escape from him. She started to run away from him. He chased her, but every time he almost caught her, he would fall in a hole, the ground would cave in.

She ran towards the mountains. As she got there she found a little hole in the side of the mountain, and in this little hole or little cave lived some *Awakkulé* [Little People]. There was one there, he was going to help her. When *Iisbishéetbishe* got to the hole he asked for the young woman, but instead the *Awakkulé* released his two pets, *bish-kakáasaache* [domestic animals] which were a mountain lion and a bear. There was a big fight but *Iisbishéetbishe* killed them both. The *Awakkulé* then attacked *Iisbishéetbishe* and killed him. He and the young woman built a big fire on the body and burned it all up.

The young woman then lived with the little people. During the days the little people would go hunting. They told her that if a little old woman would come to the door that she must not open the door for her. It was on one of these days, when the little people were gone, that the little old woman that they were talking about came to the door and knocked on the door. She knocked and knocked and called out for someone to let her in. Come to find out it was *Hísshishtawia*. She was going to kill the young woman, but just in time, the little people came home and fought *Hísshishtawia* and got the young woman back.

They ran away, and as they ran the young woman began to fall behind and she said, "Go ahead and go on without me. I am so slow, the old woman will catch up to us and eat us up. Go without me." They told her that they were not going to go on without her. They used their powers and cast her into the sky. They made the young woman a star so that *Hísshishtawia* couldn't get her. This is the story of how a young woman became Mars.

A second version of the origin of the Woman Star was told by Nathan, an elder from Lodge Grass. He gave the story a different twist, with Red Woman as the kidnapper.

The Morning Star, I heard one story about that. The Morning Star was a little girl. A little girl in the Crow Tribe. A little girl, and here she belongs to the chief. She belongs to the chief and she's a little girl. One night the woman they call *Hísshishtawia* [Red Woman], a witch, came and stole this girl, stole the little girl. She ran off with her.

The next day they started tracking her, started tracking her and kept calling her. She went across three big rivers, put down her *bachípe* [digging stick] and crossed. After the third big river she crossed, they almost caught up with her, just about caught up with her, and there was no other way she could run. So she turned around and told this one's mother, she said, "You never can get this little girl back. I'm going to send her somewhere that you can't even reach or you can't get near her." She sent that girl as high as she could, and she stopped there and stayed there.

That's the Woman Star, a Morning Star. You see, they say she was a little girl. They say after that, that's why lots of girls are named for the Morning Star, maybe Pretty Morning Star or Morning Star Girl or something like that. I said, "How come?" and they said, "because that Morning Star is a girl."

Crow people have come to define the stars of the morning and of the evening not just because they herald sunrise and sunset, but because they also incorporate important lessons for people about actions and consequences.

Chapter 5

THE TWINS AND THE HAND STAR

To describe the origin of one of the most prominent winter constellations, the Hand Star, the Crows often tell two variants of one major narrative. This group of stars are part of the Euro-American constellation Orion. The belt of Orion is seen as the wrist, his sword as the thumb, and the stars Cursa, Rigel, and SAO 132067 as the fingertips. The creation of the Hand Star is a story about the genesis of a constellation, about family unity, about the reasoning behind the sweatlodge ceremony and, finally, about the destruction of ancient evil beings in order to make the world safe for human inhabitants.

Its two main characters are the divine twins, *Baháa Awúuasshiituua*, or "Thrown Into The Spring," and *Bitáalasshiaalitchiasshiituua*, or "Thrown Behind The Tipi Lining." In this story they are credited with the origins of the sweatlodge, a ritual of spiritual and physical cleansing, but they are also seen as the originators of many other aspects of native Crow religion.

In this story the names of the Twins' parents, *Balápooshe*, the father, and *Bíashiilapee*, the mother, are interesting because of the linguistic clues they provide. *Balápooshe* was translated by two narrators of this story as "Burnt Wood," which appears to derive from

49

War shield of Two Leggings. The stylized hand in the upper left represents the Hand Star; the black line across the middle represents the dark face time, *iisanchihpashé*; and the bottom half, painted with red vermillion, represents the dawn light, mid-1800s (courtesy of the Field Museum of Natural History, Chicago, catalog #71725-2, photo by Diane A. White).

an attempt to rationalize possible components of meaning in the word: *balapé*, "wood," and *óoshee*, "cooked or burned." But other elders state that the term refers to a corn tassel and cannot be broken down phonemically. The differences may derive from the fact that the Crow's contact with a horticultural lifestyle was brief or only vicarious through their Hidatsa relatives.

When I contacted Hidatsa speakers at Ft. Berthold to see if they could provide any insights, they said the Twins' primary caretaker, a maternal uncle, was known as *Iixúalapaapish*, or "Charred Body," because he was an arrow that came down from the heavens and his body, the arrow's shaft, was burned by an evil being on this earth. I then asked if they had the term *Balápooshe*, and they said that the closest similar sounding word was *balapóoshe*, a term originally applied to hominy but presently used for a sweetened corn pudding. This term can be segmented into two terms common to both Hidatsa and Crow: *ba-* an indefinite object; and *dapóoshe*, "swollen"—hence "something (corn) that is swollen" equals "hominy." Hominy was historically prepared by stirring with a corn tassel, so the term may be a misapplication by non-horticultural Crow speakers or an attempt to translate Charred Body into the Crow language.

The task of interpreting the mother's name also produces differences of opinion. When the character Red Woman is asked by the mother what she uses as a plate, she replies, "*Bíashiilapee* is my plate." And, as in the two stories that follow, some translate the term as a pregnant woman, which would be *bíasshiilape*, while others divide the word into *bía*, meaning "woman," and *shíilapee*, an archaic term meaning "red fox" which, aside from this context, is only applied to Old Man Coyote's companion, a red fox. Therefore, the name may be translated as "Red Fox Woman."

In the first version, as told by Peter, an elder from Pryor, there is a close resemblance to the story as told by the Hidatsa. Here the nemesis of the twins is a character named *Baaáalichke*, or "One With A Long Arm," who captures Thrown Into The Spring in order to kill and eat him, since the boy had killed his relatives on earth. But instead *Baaáalichke* loses his hand to Thrown Into The Spring who then throws it up into the skies to create the Hand Star.

In the first story the mother is brought back to life by four of her personal items which include her *bíiwitche*, "mortar" and *iiwaaláhchituua*, "pestle." These two items were used to process berries to make dried berry cakes or to add to meat and fat to produce pemmican. The *bíiwitche* is a shallow bowl-shaped stone in which berries are placed and then pounded with a bell-shaped pestle, or *iiwaaláhchituua*. No longer utilized today, Crow people now process berries using hand grinders or even automatic food processors, so the terms are mostly heard these days within the narration of such old stories as the following:

> It is said that occasionally a family would leave camp, some were known to leave camp and go out on their own. They would kill buffalo, deer, and elk to get ready for the winter. When winter came they would return to their main camp.

> During this time there was a young couple who left the main camp. The husband was named *Balápooshe*. They went to a wooded area with a stream and made camp by a spring. *Balápooshe* went hunting every

A woman using a *bíiwitche* (mortar) and *iiwaaláhchituua* (pestle). Pencil drawing by Ramona Medicine Crow, 1996 (author's collection).

day even though his wife was pregnant. Though his wife was near to having her baby, he would hunt all day and return in the evenings.

One day when he went hunting and left his wife alone, an old woman approached and called, "Young lady, I came to see you." The wife said, "I am grilling meat, come in, eat." The old woman entered the tipi, she was Red Woman. Red Woman said, "I'll add wood to the fire." She added a rock instead and arranged the wood on the fire.

The wife then offered Red Woman a serving of meat in a wooden bowl. Red Woman refused saying, "This is not what I eat from." The wife thought and put the meat on a plate made of a buffalo's shoulder blade. "No, no, this is not what I eat from," said Red Woman. Then the woman put the meat on a piece of rawhide. Red Woman said, "I don't eat from this either." In frustration the wife asked, "What do you eat from?" "Pregnant women are my plate, that is what I like to eat from," replied Red Woman. The wife, being a good hostess, wished to please her visitor, so she laid down and placed the meat on her stomach.

As Red Woman ate the meat, she reached for the rock she had put in the fire. She got the hot rock and placed it on the wife's belly. It burned through the woman and killed her. Red Woman then reached into the womb and pulled out the babies, there were twins it is said. She threw one behind the lining of the tipi and the other she threw in the spring. Red Woman then placed the wife outside the door of the tipi and took a fire brand and burned her mouth at the corners to make her appear as if she were smiling. Red Woman then ran away.

As the young man neared the camp he called his wife, but there was no response. When he saw his wife beside the door smiling, he called to her but she did not answer. He realized his wife was dead and began to cry. Then he put her body on a burial scaffold and cried, mourning her death.

As he returned to the tipi he tried to figure out how she died. He found the rock that killed her, but he could not figure out why she was killed. He spent his time wandering around, mourning and fasting over his wife's death. He occasionally hunted but never returned to the main camp.

After a couple of years went by, *Balápooshe* was eating in his tipi and out of the corner of his eye he noticed something moving behind the liner of the tipi. He could not tell what it was so he moved closer until he could see a little boy. The little boy cried, "Father, let me eat." The man replied, "Go ahead, eat." A boy about two years old came out from behind the lining and ate, he ate a lot. The boy had been raised by mice it is said. *Balápooshe* wondered where the boy had come from, but he did not question him since the boy called him father.

The father continued to hunt every day, returning to camp to his son, glad to have someone with him. One day this little boy was outside playing when out of the spring emerged a little boy. They played together every day. When the father would approach, the little boy from the spring knew and he would go into the water.

One day the father made a set of arrows and a bow for his son. The next day, after the man had left, the son showed his new toys to the boy from the spring. The boy liked them and said, "Ask your father to make me a set." In the evening when the father returned, the boy from the spring jumped back in the water.

That night the son asked his father, "Can you make me another set of arrows and a bow?" The father asked why, and the boy said he wanted to shoot his arrows at one target and then when he got to that target he wanted a second set of arrows and bow to shoot back. The father was suspicious but he made the second set anyway.

Soon *Balápooshe* discovered that his son was eating a lot of food and he asked him why he was eating so much. It was then the little boy told him, "There are two of us. Red Woman killed our mother and she threw me behind the lining of the tipi and threw my twin brother in the spring and the creatures of the water have raised him, he is mean like them."

The father sat thinking about how to get the other boy back. He then took a piece of rawhide and made his son an outfit. He told him, "When I'm done you wear this and when he comes out to play arrows with you I will be hiding nearby. When he comes out of the spring and plays with you, you argue with him and when you get a chance, grab him and don't let go and I'll come running to help you."

The father built a sweatlodge. He gathered wood and prepared the wood and stones for the fire. He then returned to the camp and saw that the little boy from the spring had come out to play. The boy from the spring was looking at his brother and said, "You have a nice outfit, where did you get it?" He replied, "My father made it for me." The one from the spring said, "Ask him to make me one." He did not realize that the outfit was meant for him, so that he could not hurt his brother.

The boy from the spring sensed the man was near, he asked, "Is your father nearby?" The other replied, "No." They continued to play arrows until the one from behind the lodge lining argued over a point. As the one from the spring looked at the arrows his brother grabbed him and hollered for his father. "Father, father I got him." His father came running. The one from the spring kept trying to bite the other one, but he could not bite through the rawhide. The father grabbed him and yelled at the other son, "Run and start the sweat." *Balápooshe* took the boy into the sweat. The boy struggled to get away, he screamed, "You're burning me, father, father, you're burning me." He remembered that *Balápooshe* was his father, he remembered who he was and that he was human.

When they got out of the sweatlodge, *Balápooshe* let the boy go and he ran and tried to return to the spring, but he couldn't go in, he just sat in the water. Eventually he came back and started living with his father and brother. They went on, the boys played and the father went hunting every day. The boys were called *Baháa Awúuasshiituuash*, Thrown Into The Spring, and *Bitáalasshiaalitchiasshiituuash*, Thrown Behind The Tipi Lining.

One day Thrown Into The Spring asked, "Where's our mother?" His twin replied, "Don't say that, our mother is dead." Thrown Into The Spring said, "Why didn't you tell me, I can bring her back to life." The other twin said, "Don't say that." He replied, "No I can, let's go."

They went and got her hatchet, her *iiwaaláhchituua* [pestle], *bíiwitche* [mortar], and comb. Thrown Into The Spring told his twin, "Watch her when she comes to life and sits up and reaches out her hand, grab her hand, try to grab her hand. If you don't get her hand it won't be good. Try hard to grab her hand."

They went to the scaffold. Thrown Into The Spring took the hatchet and threw it, hollering, "Mother, your hatchet might cut you." The scaffold moved a little, then he grabbed the *iiwaaláhchituua* and threw it, yelling, "Mother, your *iiwaaláhchituua* is going to hit you." The scaffold again moved, he then grabbed the *bíiwitche* and threw it, saying, "Mother, your *bíiwitche* is going to hit you." The scaffold moved harder. Then he grabbed the comb and threw it, hollering, "Mother, get up and comb your hair" and she sat up. Thrown Behind The Tipi Lining grabbed her hand and helped her up. The boys hugged her and brought her back to camp.

As the father was returning to camp the twins ran to greet him, he said, "Why are you so happy, you are not usually like this." They replied, "Our mother is here." He told them not to say that, that their mother was dead. Thrown Behind The Tipi Lining replied, "No, Thrown Into The Spring brought her back to life and she is at the camp." They went and the father greeted her.

The mother started telling the twins of the bad things that were around. She told them about the bear that kills all that comes near. She said, "Over in a patch of berries lives a bear that is very dangerous, don't go near it." The boys were older now and they wished to explore. Thrown Into The Spring said, "Why don't we go see this bear our mother talked about, I wonder if it is true or not." His brother agreed.

The two went to the berry patch where the bear lived. The bear spotted the boys and said, "I eat all that comes near me." The boys said, "We are here to kill you. It is not right that you kill everything and anything." The bear charged at Thrown Behind The Tipi Lining, but Thrown Into The Spring shot him through the head with an arrow. They then piled wood on the bear and burned it up. This is why bears only charge and kill occasionally.

The boys went home and told their mother what they had done. The mother was surprised and told the boys that they should not have gone there, then she said, "There is a treacherous cougar and I want you to stay away from it, it kills everything within sight." The next day as the brothers played, Thrown Into The Spring asked his brother, "Do you think that cougar our mother told us about is dangerous? Maybe we should go see."

They went to the foothills and found the cougar. The cougar growled at the boys and Thrown Into The Spring said, "Don't fool around." But the cougar rushed him and he shot it through the head. They then put wood on its body and burned it all up. This is why cougars stay in the mountains and rarely kill people.

The boys returned to their mother, telling her what they had done and she scolded them, "You should listen to me and not do the opposite of what I say. Now I am going to tell you about an elk who has captured the winds. When he opens his mouth people fly into it, so don't go near him." Again the boys pondered their mother's comments and wondered if the elk was really dangerous. They decided to go see it.

As they neared where the elk lived they could hear it breathing. They called to it and it sucked them in. Inside the elk's stomach they found many people who had been sucked in before them. The boys talked about how they could get out and Thrown Into The Spring said he would cut them out. He touched the elk's heart and asked, "What is this?" And the elk said, "That is what I plan with, don't touch it." The boy took his knife and cut off the heart and the elk fell dead. He then cut through the stomach and they got out.

The twins went to sleep and when Thrown Behind The Tipi Lining woke up he found his twin gone. He searched and searched for his twin, but he was nowhere to be found. He could not even find any tracks, his tracks he could see, but his brother's tracks he could not see. He thought about it and he figured that it must have been *Baaáal-ichke* [One With A Long Arm] who took him. He looked to the sky and saw a hole. He then shot his arrows and where his arrows went he went. When he got to the sky, he found a camp and life there. He came to a tipi at the outer edge of a big camp.

The tipi belonged to an old woman who was the moon. He said, "Grandmother, I've come, I belong to no one so I've come to you." She said, "Good, I belong to no one too, you stay here with me." They ate and he stayed with her. That evening he could hear drumming and singing going on, he asked, "Grandmother what are they doing." She said, "*Baaáalichke* brought Thrown Into The Spring from the earth and they are preparing him. They are going to eat him tomorrow morning." He said, "Grandmother, let's go and have a small piece too and watch." She said, "Let's go." On their way he picked up a small rock and carried it along.

The singing was taking place in a large lodge. When they got to where the singing was taking place, there was his twin almost dead, moaning and groaning. They sat at the edge of the lodge. His twin had his eyes closed and was moaning and groaning. *Baaáalichke* had his arms held around him and was squeezing him. Thrown Into The Spring looked up and saw his brother, he said, "Where did you come from?" Thrown Behind The Tipi Lining said, "Do you think I would sit here and let you die like this?"

He jumped up and threw his rock down, and said, "Let him go." *Baaáalichke* said, "Why should I?" He said, "If you don't I will do to you what I'm going to do to this rock." He took his bow and arrow and kept shooting it until it exploded into pieces. *Baaáalichke* dropped the twin. Thrown Behind The Tipi Lining helped his twin up and put him on his shoulder and took him to the opening in the sky. He threw his arrows, which took them back to earth.

Thrown Behind The Tipi Lining put his brother down on the ground. Then *Baaáalichke* reached down from the sky and tried to pick up Thrown Into The Spring, but Thrown Into The Spring cut the hand off at the wrist and it hit the ground. Then Thrown Into The Spring threw the hand back to the sky where it became the Hand Star. Thrown Into The Spring said, "You will no longer eat or destroy others. Your hand in the sky will be a symbol for all time of your cruelty." And that is how the Hand Star came to be. All the bad things that had been around to bother them had been killed. The boys returned to their father's camp and they told him what happened. He said, "It is bad all these things happening to us. Let's go back to the main camp." That is how the Hand Star came to be created.

In the second version of this story, as told by Lloyd, an elder from Crow Agency, it is the destruction of the wicked Red Woman which creates this prominent constellation:

The Hand Star. We can start with this story, I'll go over it in this manner. This story, as they call it in the Crow version, *Apsáalooke* version is, *Baháa Awúuasshiituua* was Thrown Into The Spring, *Bitáalasshi-aalitchiasshiituua*, Thrown Behind The Tipi Lining. That's the way the story is referred to in our legends.

I heard this story many times, from my grandparents. The legend of this particular star kind of has a beginning with what they call *Hissh-ishtawia* [Red Woman]. There's a name in there, *Balápooshish*. *Balápooshish* is the father of these twins, that's what he's called. *Balápooshish* is something pertaining to wood. Like an object of wood that is burned. Perhaps, it's used for an ornament or a tool. It's something pertaining to wood.

Okay, where we are on this, the way I heard the story. When I was about five or six years old, I think that's when I first heard this story. As I remember, my grandmother told this in this fashion that, long time ago, I guess, different families would go out hunting. That's how they survived, that's what they do, long time ago.

This man, *Balápooshish*, as they call him. *Balápooshish* was out hunting around one day. His wife was expecting, she was expecting. Anyhow, she stayed home. Woman is the caretaker of the home. She manages the home for everyone's comfort and that kind of thing. While the man goes out, brings in game, and other things that are needed. The women provide the wood, taking care of the home, in that fashion. While she was still at this, *Balápooshish* went out to hunt one day. In the meantime, this treacherous lady her name is *Hisshishtawia*, Red Woman, had been observant of this family. She would kind of size out the time of, during the day her husband would be away for a long time until the end of the day, he would come home, bring game, and that kind of thing.

So she already made some plans of her own that she would visit this place. She was treacherous, *Hisshishtawia*, was a treacherous woman.

Anyhow, as the husband left, shortly afterwards she came in, she came in. She came in and addressed her. She came by because she was hungry, she was hungry. Being the good hostess of those times, she was glad to have a visitor. She was going about doing her home-related chores, busy at it, doing. But she was slow getting around because of her condition. In the meantime, Red Woman brought a rock, and threw it into the fire to get it hot. That rock was in the fire.

She was cooking and everything. Finally, the meal was cooked and everything was ready, and it's time to eat, time to eat. So, she prepared a real nice tray made out of rawhide, *baattáche* [rawhide], neat and clean and everything. She placed it in front of her, Red Woman, says that's not her, she doesn't use such things to put her food on. So woman tried other things. Made other trays, bring them to her, out of wood, many things. She turned each one down. After several rejections of her generosity, of being good to the guest, well then she finally ran out of things to provide her with a tray to put the food on. So she finally says, "Well, what do you eat from with food on?" So, Red Woman says, "*Bíasshiilapee. Bíasshiilapee* is my style of eating food." Meaning a pregnant woman. The lady says, "Well, if that's the way you want it." Then she took off her garb, laid in front of her and put the food on her stomach. Red Woman pretended she was eating, enjoying.

In the meantime, she reached into the fire and got that piece of rock that she threw in there. It was red hot. She dropped it on top of the wife, where her heart was. It burned and killed her. From there Red Woman took her knife out and cut open the wife, took out, there were two, two boys, they say. Red Woman threw one behind the tipi lining and she threw the other one into the spring. Then she placed the woman and propped her up with sticks and made her face the direction that her husband always comes home. Then Red Woman burned the woman's upper lip, up here [pointing to his philtrum] so it appeared like she was smiling. That's the way the story goes, she was standing up and smiling. So, she left. Red Woman, the treacherous Red Woman left.

So at the end of the day her husband came home, her husband came home. Of course, he was anxious, thinking that there'll be a hot meal waiting for him, and he was expected. Of course he greeted her with good greeting words, as he came home. And she stood there smiling, not doing anything. As he came close to her, he touched her and she fell over. He could see where she was cut up, where Red Woman pulled out the two twins. And from there he grieved, just had a bad time. All throughout the—for a good period.

After he put her to rest somewhere nearby. He hadn't recovered from the grief, but he still would go out every day like he always did. Then one day he came home and he was preparing things for himself, of course he was sad. Then he heard a voice, he heard a voice from behind the tipi lining. The voice called for his dad. The man says,

"Whatever you are, you come out and join me in a meal." So, pretty soon there was noise, rustling going on behind the tipi lining, comes out a little boy. He greeted the little boy and right away he wasn't sure if this was his little boy or not, but it was a little boy. He called him dad right away, father. They went about their daily activities from there on. And every day he would prepare things for him, like most little boys play with.

He told him that there are a lot of bad things around, always be careful, always stay close to home. He would play. During the day the man would go out again. So, one day he came home, he came back and as the story goes, when this little boy told him, "*Axée* [address term for father], fix me another set of arrows like you did." His father told him, "One set is good enough for you, one set of arrows. Why do you want two?" And the little boy says, "Well, I'm going to place the arrows on one end, and place the other one at the other end, and play with my arrows, and get to the other end. Back and forth type of game." And so, he was questioning him on that, but he went ahead and prepared him some arrows.

In the meantime, when his dad would be away, Thrown Into The Spring would come out and the two would play together, they would play together, like children do. At the end of the day it was getting to a point where Thrown Into the Spring would sense it when the father would be coming home. When the father comes home he would say to his twin brother, "*Díilapxalitdiik*" [it smells like your father], which means, "It smells like your father is coming." Then he would jump back into the spring.

So, that went on for a long time, then finally, his father was getting suspicious, because he knew that every time he prepared him something to play with, or something to eat, he would ask to make another portion of it, double. Thinking that since he was growing, he was eating more. The play things that he had, he wanted two of them. So he was getting suspicious. And finally one day, he says, "Why are you asking me to fix an extra one of the play things, as well as the food, all this? You must have a reason. That there's not just one, there must be two of you." Finally the one, Thrown Behind The Tipi Lining, says, "Yes, my brother lives in the spring, but he's got like water creatures now. He has characteristics of sharp teeth, and those kind of things, that he could be a treacherous person. When you'd come home he would always jump back into the spring. When you leave he would come out and we would play together." So, the man says, "Well, one of these days we'll have to work something out, work something out, where we can get him back."

So, the man prepared himself, out of rawhide, gloves, leggings, and clothing made out of rawhide, so when his sharp teeth would try to bite, they won't penetrate. He already prepared that. He fixed one for his son too. He says, "When you're playing with arrows, go back and forth. You keep playing, and I'll hide nearby and I'll keep an eye on you. And as you're doing this argue with him."

Playing with arrows is a game where who has the closest to the target arrow gets a point, that's how they play the game. So, he says, "Argue with him that your arrow is closer. And if it is, both are almost identical to who has this point, a score, argue with him on it. If he argues with you on it, ask him to get real close and study it, to see if your arrow or his arrow is closer, to examine it close. As he does this," he says, "you grab him, you grab him and wrestle him to the ground. That way we'll get him back." So, he agreed. So, he fixed him one too. He liked the outfit that was made out of rawhide. He says, "Ask your father to make one for me too." He didn't know that it was for him, in case he gets vicious.

So, in the meantime he already had the sweatlodge ready and everything. *Balápooshish*, the father. So, he was watching them play, and after a long while of playing the game, they got to a point where they were arguing to whose arrow was closer to the target arrow. "I think I beat you on that one." He says, "No, I beat you." You know how kids come to argue on who's winning over whom. So he told him to get down and examine it real close, because his arrow was closer than his, and that kind of thing. So, he got down to, like he had anticipated, like he had planned. He got down to examine it real close, and at that time, he grabbed him. So, right away, he attacked him, and tried to bite his clothes, his arms, and everything, and it wouldn't penetrate.

So he hollered out, "Father I got him, I got him!" So, he come running out, and they wrestled him. He was powerful, they said, he was strong, he had the characteristics of the water creatures now. He was strong and vicious. So, they wrestled him to the ground, and they tied him up, they tied him up, they tied his arms and legs. He kept hollering and screaming, and all that, but they kept tying him. They got the sweat bath real hot and they took him in, they took him in. *Balápooshish* was pouring water on, he kept the sweat going hot. Thrown Into The Spring kept hollering, hollering. Then, finally he called him, "Father! Father! I'm over it now. I'm over it now." The bad omen that he'd acquired being in the water, with the water creatures. So, they brought him out of it. When he come out, he was normal. They were normal kids then. So he was happy because the two boys were twins.

They were going about and they're quite adventurous. They were adventurous, the two boys. Their arrows were like magic. When they're traveling, they would shoot their arrows, and wherever they'd go, wherever they would land, that's where they'd land. They would travel pretty fast. They had magical powers. Supernatural powers. All of them did.

After, they go around doing their boy adventure-type activities. One day he would tell them never to go visit this area. There's a lot of bad things over there. Don't go there because of the bad omen, and things like this. The two boys would help each other, and they would go, and they would destroy those bad things, they kept doing that.

Finally one day their father told them, "Don't go near this pond, where there is a beaver that has a tail like a knife, the edge of the tail is as sharp as a knife." He would use the tail to cut things. "He'll cut you to pieces." So, the two boys, they kind of thought about it. "Whoever wants to go look for a beaver with a bad tail, treacherous tail?" So they went looking for that pond. They finally found it.

They have magic arrows, and so on, and so they kind of approached the beaver with kindness. The beaver was trying to be kind too, but in the meantime he was going to cut them into pieces with his tail. But they were always alert, very cautious. Finally, as the beaver was in the position to cut them, they'd jump to one side. As this was going on, the other one killed him. They cut off the tail, and the tail was to their advantage, because they can cut with it, all the other bad things. So they wanted to use that beaver's tail to go around destroying all the other bad things that were about. They got rid of them, monsters, and all the bad things that were there. They use that beaver's magic tail to cut to pieces the treacherous things that were about.

So, one day they felt that they got enough powers, they got enough powers. And one of them says, "Let's go look for treacherous woman, the woman that killed our mother. Let's see if we can find her, and make her pay for the bad deed that she brought on the family." So, that one day they went seeking out, as their father went out.

The story goes, they went looking for treacherous woman, Red Woman, and they found her. And she was trying to impress the boys that she was a kind lady and all that, but they knew better. As she was trying to use her magic on the two boys. They had their magic arrows and everything. And they start using that beaver's tail on her, they start injuring her. So she screamed, and she ran all over the place, and they chased her, and they chased her. They kept cutting parts of her body, as she was running. As she was running all over the place, screaming.

Finally, most of her limbs were cut off already, and the two boys were right behind her with that beaver's tail. And in desperation, in desperation, she reached for the skies. She wants to get away from these two, two twins, because they would destroy her. So she reached for the skies. As she reached for the sky, her hand got up, but the boys went and cut at the wrist, before she could reach for the sky. So she fell down, and they cut her to pieces, but her hand's still up there, her hand, *Ihkawaléische* [Hand Star]. Her hand's still up there. But the rest of her was destroyed and they say that all the red ground you see around the foot of the mountains, that's her blood, from when she was running.

And so the boys came home, and they said, "Well, let's bring our mother back to life, because she's been dead for too long. Now that we've destroyed the lady, the treacherous woman that destroyed our mother. We destroyed her. Now we'll bring our mother back." The other one says, "How can we do that?" He says, "Well, we'll use our arrows." So they come and visit the place where their mother was, and one boy shot his arrow skyward. He says, "*Ihkáa* [address term for mother], *Ihkáa*, you better get up and start taking care of your home. Without you, there is no one to take care of us." She moved when they said this. The next arrow they shot they said, "Mother, your cooking is almost complete. It's almost cooked." At that time, she sat up. The next arrow that they shot, they said, "Mother, you better get up now, your cooking is boiling." She stood up.

So the next arrow they said, "Mother, you better get up now, your cooking is boiling over." So that arrow brought her back to life. She went about and she was cooking and preparing things. As each arrow was shot up, it kept getting higher, higher. They were taking turns doing this. As the next arrow went up, so they brought her back to life, according to the story. She come back into life and she was up and going about preparing things.

All during that time, she got everything ready for the home, and everything was back to normal, and their father come home that one evening. And there was a lot of happiness in the home. The two boys were out there playing, enjoying themselves, and their mother was preparing meals, and taking care of the home, their father come home to a regular, normal home, where the two boys were happy and she was happy. Everything was back to normal, type of thing. In the meantime, during that period from the time that they were thrown into the spring, in behind the wall and that kind of thing, finally up to the time they got rid of all the bad, treacherous things that were there. And, also they got rid of Red Woman.

The moral of it is that, in desperation she reached for the sky. They use that as when a person is running out of things. *Awáxichisshe dúuchiichik* [grasping at the roots of the sky] means, there's no other place to turn to, but the sky. Once they do that they're already destroyed. That's what it means, you're desperate to try anything that even offers the last hope.

When it relates to the sweatlodge, the sweat bath is a way of getting rid of any kind of bad omen, and things that are within, and it brings out the goodness. So, the sweatlodge practice comes from one of the stories. This is one of them. Cleansing, and then, the spirituality. It brings out all that. Gets rid of the bad things within a person. So, there's morality in those practices. In association with stars, today you look at the Hand Star. It reminds you of that story.

This prominent constellation teaches the strength of a family's love, the significance of religious practices, and the desperation of individuals who act in improper or immoral ways. The lessons of the stars are ever present.

Chapter 6

THE SEVEN STARS

In the Northern Hemisphere the most visible constellation is the circumpolar constellation commonly known as the Big Dipper. These seven stars are very important to the Crow people. They are considered to be seven brothers, or seven brothers and a sister, or sometimes seven buffalo bulls. The leader of the seven brothers is named "Black Wolf," *Cheétshipitash*, and the youngest is known as "Cedar Between The Eyes," *Ischéenmuluxpawishe*, or *Iiwakkuluush*.

To the Crow, Black Wolf is seen as a war leader or *Iipche Akkuleé*, "Pipe Carrier," as the Crow term it, since the symbol of his office is a pipe. The youngest is viewed as a young man with a cedar chip above the bridge of the nose. His other name, *Iiwakkuluush*, can no longer be translated by Crows, but Hidatsa speakers told me the term means "breast bone or sternum," with *iiwakki* meaning "chest" and *huluu* meaning "a bone."

The Seven Brothers are also believed to have been responsible for bringing two enemy war parties together on the open plains, so that they might eat the flesh of those killed in the ensuing battle. Others have attributed this role to only Cedar Between The Eyes. Ben, an elder from the Pryor District, related that all the bodies of the dead are taken by this individual to be eaten. In this last capacity, Cedar Between The Eyes was said to be a servant to the Morning Star. As he explained:

The war leader's pipe bowl of Standing Bull. The seven saucer shaped indentations in the top of the bowl represent the Seven Stars (Big Dipper), and the lines represent the stars in general, mid-1800s (courtesy of the National Museum of the American Indian, Smithsonian Institution, catalog #11/7698, photo by Pam Dewey).

> *Ihkaléaxe* [Morning Star] has a helper, and this helper is supposed to be a giant, a huge man. They call him *Ischéenmuluxpawishe* [Cedar Between The Eyes]. They say he has a cedar chip between his eyes, so that's why they call him *Ischéenmuluxpawishe*. He is the one that takes the dead people back to the Other Side, or where they go when they die. They attribute cannibalistic tendencies; they say that this man, this giant, *Ischéenmuluxpawishe*, he eats the dead people and that's why they fear him. He has cannibalistic tendencies.

Cannibalism is associated with other supernatural beings of the Crow, and is not necessarily indicative of an evil being. In the following story it is two benevolent beings, White Owl and his wife, who are shown to practice cannibalism.

This narrative centers around the exploits of the famous Yellow Leggings. Among other things, Yellow Leggings learned from White Owl how to construct and respect the tipi. Oral tradition states that before Yellow Leggings' encounter with White Owl, as described below, the Crow lived in the shelter of rock overhangs.

Aside from overcoming a treacherous elk and killing the evil Red Hair and his mother, Yellow Leggings also meets with three half human/half animal seductresses who are still believed to inhabit various parts of the Crow Reservation. In human form they are exceedingly beautiful, easily able to seduce a man. Should one fall under their spell, however, he will be driven crazy.

It is said that a particular homeless individual on the reservation is thought to have been seduced by a were-otter, thus providing a rationale for his odd behavior. Hunters lost in the mountains are often said to be victims of were-elk. White tail deer are also thought to be capable of this transformation. Once, my Crow father came to visit me and my wife shortly after we purchased a home in an area known for its were-white tail deer. After surveying the property and giving his general approval, he laughingly instructed me to stay indoors at dusk and dawn for it is at these times that were-white tail roamed about. He further said that should I be alone, outside, during these times, that I should not go to someone calling my name or approach mysteriously appearing women. People routinely take precautions against meeting were-animals.

In the following story, Yellow Leggings is not only attracted by all three types of were-animals, but, more importantly, he is able to overcome them and find his appropriate wife, the sister of the Seven Brothers. The story concludes with the brothers deciding to become stars, in order to be able to protect the Crow forever. And if any Crow should decide to pray to them, the Seven Brothers would grant whatever is desired. This last point was brought home when Kirk, an elder from Reno, advised me to pray to the Seven Brothers. When suffering a crisis, he said, "Take a cigarette and plead to them day or night. They're up there, they'll help you."

This manner of communicating with the Big Dipper through a tobacco "smoke" accounts for one of the other commonly heard Crow names for this constellation, *Iipchalapaachuoo*, or the "Pipe Pointer Stars."

THE SEVEN BROTHERS

The first version of this story was provided by Lloyd, an elder from the Black Lodge District:

> Our stories are in association with everything that's about, some of them pertain to the stars. The most obvious stars we call the Seven Stars, or *Ihkasáhpua*, or they refer to it as where you point your pipe—*Iipchalapaachuoo*. *Iipchalapaachuoo* means that's where you point your pipe, offering good things to the heavenly bodies. These are experiences of the one we call Yellow Leggings, *Issaatshíile*.

> Yellow Leggings liked to trap eagles. He'd skin a rabbit for bait, dig a hole to sit in and cover it with brush. He'd wait for an eagle to come along to eat the rabbit. Then he'd reach up and grab the feet. He'd take the good feathers, the two middle feathers and let the eagle go.

> This man, Yellow Leggings, went to catch eagles. He waited a long time. He heard noises like an eagle coming. He waited, waited, but then the pit was dark. He put his hand up and felt a rock or boulder covering the pit. He was trapped by a rock rolling over the hole. He tried to move it, push it out. He pushed on it but he couldn't move the rock. Then he saw a mouse at one end of the pit. He begged the mouse for help. The mouse took him to a hole. The hole looked too small for him to fit, but he pushed his way in and he could pull himself along. Then it got bigger, so he could crawl, then stoop, and finally stand up. Once he could stand he started to run. He came out of the tunnel and found himself in a new land.

> He looked around; he was lost. It was a different place, some other place, not this earth. He walked around. Then he saw a white tipi.

Inside was an old man. This man's name is White Owl. He invited Yellow Leggings to come in and sit beside him. The man's wife gave Yellow
Leggings some soup, but he saw a human hand swirling in the pot. The
old man said, "Humans don't eat that type of food, they don't eat it."

He told Yellow Leggings he wants him to do something for him, he
wants him to kill a treacherous elk. He says, "This elk is very dangerous. It has helpers that watch it when he sleeps. He's very dangerous."
White Owl gave him one arrow and says, "You have to kill the elk with
this one arrow, you have just one chance."

Yellow Leggings went outside and began to cry because he knows the
elk is very dangerous. He cries and cries until a snowbird comes to
him and says the elk could be killed with the help of moles. He goes to
the moles' home and asks for help. The leader of these moles agrees
and says he will dig a tunnel under the elk so he can get to his heart.
To kill the elk with one arrow, he has to shoot him in the heart. As the
mole digs the hole, they can hear the elk's heart pounding. Yellow Leggings fired at his heart and the elk jumped up and pushed his antler
into the ground. Yellow Leggings ran down the tunnel, but the elk's
right behind him. Just as Yellow Leggings feels the antler in his back,
the elk dies. Yellow Leggings cuts off the antler tip on the front. That's
what White Owl wanted, the antler tip. He returns to White Owl with
the antler tip.

Now, White Owl tells him he wants him to get the head of *Isshiiooshé*
[Red Hair]. *Isshiiooshé* means kind of like burned hair, red hair.
Again, Yellow Leggings cried and the snowbird comes to him and tells
him to go to Ant Woman, she can help him. He goes to her tipi and Ant
Woman tells him that she would help him because Red Hair is always
bothering her, asking her to marry him.

She says they can change bodies to fool Red Hair so he can get close to
him, so he can kill him. They rubbed their bodies together all over.
This way they changed bodies. So now Yellow Leggings has Ant
Woman's body. She also gives him a louse to put in the place of Red
Hair's head. Red Hair lives with his mother on an island. Ant Woman
gives Yellow Leggings corn pemmicans and tells him, "When you get to
the water there will be a *bishkahpisée*, [big-eared dog]. The dog will be
waiting for you on your way. When you straddle the dog, he'll swim
across this wide body of water. He'll take you across this lake, this
large body of water. He'll take you across to this island. When the dog
is paddling along, and when he tires out, feed him a pemmican, put a
corn pemmican in the corner of his mouth. To pick up his strength
again." So, he did that, all of that, and the dog took him to the island
where Red Hair and his mother live.

Then finally when he comes to this dwelling, that's their home. The
mother was suspicious when she saw Ant Woman, since she never
married her son in the past. But Red Hair wants her for his wife, so he
tells her to be quiet.

That night they lay together. Red Hair kept making advances, but Yellow Leggings played him off. When he finally falls asleep, Yellow Leggings cuts his head off and puts the louse on the pillow. The mother kept asking if Red Hair was okay, since she was suspicious. The louse would answer, "Be quiet. I'm alive." But the louse got weaker and weaker with each answer, so by the fourth time the louse could hardly speak. The mother jumped up and went to the bed and pulls the covers back sees her dead son and Ant Woman was gone.

She ran after Ant Woman, but Yellow Leggings had already crossed back across the water and gone into Ant Woman's tipi. The treacherous woman got to the tipi. This woman has a hook on the forehead, not a hook but a spearlike thing on her head, *iiwíaxittua*. *Iiwíaxittua* means like this [he draws a picture of an arrow point]. This is the *iiwíaxittua*, that's what they refer to as *iiwíaxittua*. She uses that to destroy things. In the meantime, Yellow Leggings went inside. He and Ant Woman were inside the rock dwelling. They were safe. So, this thing, this woman would go up real high, then come down and would hit the rock, the rock dwelling. It would chip off. Each time she'd do that, Ant woman would wet the hole with her saliva and patch it. Each place she hit, Ant Woman would spit on her hand and fix the hole.

The mother finally realizes that she can't penetrate the tipi, she couldn't break up the rock dwelling. So she pleaded to just have her son's head. She said, "If I could just have my son's head I will leave you alone. Let me look at my son, let me look at my son's head. Just let me look at his face." But they know she's going to try to trick them into letting her in so she can destroy them. So, they place the head in the center of the tipi where it can be seen.

Ant Woman opens the door, just open up wide enough for her to peek her head in. As the mother tries to put her head in she says, "I tricked you, now I'm going to kill you." But when she put her head in, at that moment, they closed the door. Chopped off her head. So, he destroyed them. They then changed bodies back by touching all over, but they missed the armpits. That's why women's armpits are larger, more muscular, than men's.

Yellow Leggings took the heads to White Owl. On his way back he was instructed that when he approaches this man with all the sacred objects, meaning White Owl, that he'll lay out all his sacred things. As he points out each one and describes how certain things can be used, he'll ask you to pick one. "Which one do you want to use? Which one do you want to take?" And you say to him, "I want you." He can't back away, he'll have to help you. Because you brought him the heads, he'll have to help you.

When Yellow Leggings returns to White Owl's tipi, he does as he was told. White Owl agrees. He gives him all his powers, including a fawn and an owl. The owl represents him. As Yellow Leggings was leaving, White Owl tells him to be careful because four women will approach him. The first three will be treacherous, but the fourth will become his wife.

As he went, he came to a beautiful woman. He lay with her, but she jumped up and ran away. He saw she was an otter. The second one, same thing, but it was a deer, and the third, an elk. The fourth one was a woman, a human, and he lay with her but she didn't fear him, so she became his wife.

This woman had seven brothers. But her brothers were supernatural, they had special powers is what it is. So, they're his brothers-in-law, there were seven of them. The youngest was Cedar Between The Eyes and he had a pet bear and mountain lion. When Yellow Leggings and his new wife went to her home, the youngest was there, the others were away. When the others came home, they teased Yellow Leggings. They pulled off their heads and other parts of their bodies and threw them about. Yellow Leggings got out his fawn and owl, and the owl grabbed the fawn and as it squeezed the fawn the brothers hollered in pain. They pleaded with their sister to make Yellow Leggings stop, and he called back his owl.

Cedar Between The Eyes told his brothers, "I'm ashamed of you. You should respect your brother-in-law." And he gave Yellow Leggings his bear as a gift. This began the custom of giving a gift to your new brother-in-law, to show respect.

Now that bad things were destroyed, they decided to become something that would be there forever. So, they had a meeting among themselves. "What shall we become, so we can last forever?" And suggestions were, "Why don't we become wood, trees?" "But trees die." "Why don't we become rocks high in the mountains?" "Rocks from erosion will fall." "Why don't we become water?" "Oh, water sometimes, it will dry up, from the heat and all that kind of thing." So, they had a long discussion on this, and finally one of them says, "Why don't we become where they point the pipe stem to the stars? We can be there for forever, and that way, we can watch the *Bíiluuke* forever." So they said, "That's a good idea."

They say that the youngest brother took his pet. They say the mountain lion is up there. That is why there's a little star next to the handle, it's Cedar Between The Eyes' pet, according to the story I heard. So that's when they become the seven stars. They become the Big Dipper. So, that's where the idea that they become the stars. Every time you offer prayers to the east, to the south, to the west, to the north, groundward, upward, and then finally yourself. Seven of them, seven times that you do this. The spirit is within you too.

You remind yourself of the spiritual connection that you have with the Seven Brothers. That they have power. And they say that the pipe actually comes from the heavens too. But that's where the term *Iipchala-*

paachuoo [Pipe Pointer Stars], where they point the pipe stem comes from, the Seven Stars, according to that story.

In the next variant of this story, the sister joins her brothers in the sky, the lead brother becoming Polaris, the North Star, around whom his siblings will circle for eternity. This version of the story was told by Inez, an elder from Lodge Grass:

> This one about the Seven Stars must be the one that is called Pipe Pointer Stars. I will tell you what I know about the Big Dipper. There will be others who will tell this story each in their own way. This is my version of the way I heard it.
>
> There were seven brothers. Their parents were either dead or just were not mentioned in this story. There were seven brothers and a little sister, which was the youngest of them all. At this time their food was running low. One of the young men said, "I should get us some meat," and he went to hunt. They waited for him. They waited and waited, but he did not come back for several days. One of the brothers said, "Something must have happened to him, because he should have been back by now. Maybe he got hurt or something." He said, "I will go and check on him and find out what has happened." He went to find his brother, but he also never came back. So another brother went to check and so on, until only one brother was left with the little sister.
>
> He hated to leave his little sister alone. Finally, he told her, "We have no other choice. If I stay, we will die of hunger." He spoke to his little sister and explained to her how to take care of their home and how to take care of herself while he was gone.
>
> He started out full of hope, looking for his brothers. He went on and on until he came to a place where he saw a tipi and a young man came out to greet him. He said, "We knew that you would be coming, so we were waiting for you. You are going on a journey that I wouldn't advise. There is a woman that took your brothers. She is keeping them hostage and making slaves of them. She is very dangerous. On the way back from your journey, if you should make it, this woman has her medicine, a *bachipe* [digging stick] with her at all times since it is the only means of getting what she wants. She never separates herself from it. Remember, she is a dangerous woman. Now as you go on, you will come to another home. There you will receive more instructions."
>
> So this last brother continued on his journey, until he came to the home that he was told about. There he was told, "My son, this is a dangerous journey that you are taking. She has kept your brothers captive, and they are very skinny now, from the lack of food." He made four arrows for him, one yellow, one black, one blue, and the other red. "If she should come out of her dwelling place to do work or to go for water, you need to wait until she is out of sight. This is the only chance you have to save yourselves. If you make it, she eats by herself and gives only small portions to the brothers, and they barely have any

meat on them. They are very poor. Take one of these arrows and you will come to the place she lives. Go along following the arrow to where it meets with the ground. Do the same thing with the others, and you will make it. [By throwing the arrows he would travel with them and they would take him to his destination.] Now, when you come to this river, there lives an old woman."

After he was given the instructions, and given the four arrows, this last brother went on his way. He reached the place of the old woman. She said, "Oh dear, I knew this would happen, I knew you would come, though I hoped you wouldn't." She gave this young man some corn pemmican, and told him, "As you go along, you will come to a large river. There you will see a *bishkahpisée* [big-eared dog]. He will be hanging around the river's edge. While this *bishkahpisée* is going back and forth, get one of your corn pemmican and feed it to him. Just put it in the side of the mouth, and say to him, 'Take me to the other side of the river' and he will. If you ask him to wait for you, he will be there when you return. If you give him another pemmican, he will bring you back to this side of the river upon your request. Now as this *bishkah-pisée* brings you back to this side of the river, about the time that you reach this side, the woman will have caught up with you. When she puts her *bachípe* across the river, she will climb it to get to you. As she does this, grab the end of her medicine and turn it over as she gets to the middle of the river, and she will fall. As she falls into the river, say 'Father, here is what you wanted to eat.' If you do this just as I have told you, you will be safe. On the other hand if you make one mistake, she will get you."

The young man left with the instructions he was given. Just as the old woman told him, he saved and watched the corn pemmican very closely. When he got to the edge of the river, sure enough the *bishkah-pisée* was on the edge of the river walking back and forth. The young man got one of his corn pemmican and fed it to him. He put it in the side of his mouth and asked him, "Take me across the river." The *bishkahpisée* took him across just as the old woman told him it would. The young man asked the *bishkahpisée* to wait for him there, that he would return.

When he got to the place that his brothers were, this woman saw him and said, "As if they would live through this, as if they could make it." The young man went into the place his brothers were. They were very thin, as he was told, and they were all there. The woman held them captive there. The brothers waited and watched. The woman went outside to do some work. They waited for a little while, then peeked out of the door. She had gone out of sight. The young man said to his brothers, "We need to get out of here." They said, "No, that woman is dangerous."

But this young man was persistent. He said, "Let's go now." So they started out. As they started out, he shot his arrow, and they followed.

They repeated this till they came to the river. There waited the *bish-kahpisée*. They fed him the pemmican just as they spotted the woman coming over the horizon. They got to the *bishkahpisée* and fed him the pemmican, saying, "Take us to the other side of the river." He took all of them to the other side. They got to the other side of the river, and the woman was now at the middle. As she was climbing along, the brothers turned over the *bachípe* and as she was yelling at them, she fell into the river.

The young man threw the last arrow and they made it home. He said, "This woman is dangerous, and if she comes out of the water after us we won't be safe. Let's not stay here." The other replied, "Well, what do you think we should do?" One of them said, "Let's be trees. A tree that is full of big branches like the ones that cast a big shadow." The little sister said, "My mother uses wood that she gathers for fire wood. We won't last there." One of them said, "Let's be water in the river." Again the little sister said, "My mother uses water for tanning hides. That won't be a sure thing."

Another brother said, "Well, let's become stones and be way up high in the mountains." The little sister says, "My mother uses rock to scrape the hides that she gets. She breaks them to use, and many of them become as sharp as knives." "Well, think of something," said another. One replies, "On this earth lies all evil things. Let's become where they point the pipes." The others say, "What is that?" and he says, "The stars." The others said, "But stars fall." But he said, "We will hold each other and not fall. We will be forever." They all started out after dark, on their journey.

It is said that these Seven Brothers are what is today called the Big Dipper. On the handle just to the side of it there is a little star, and that one is the little sister with her puppy. On a clear night you can go out and you can see it. They have a home there. Her, her little puppy, and her seven brothers. They are forever I am told.

   This final discussion of how the Seven Brothers decide to become the Big Dipper is a favorite aspect of the story. Nathan, an elder whose grandfather was a renowned storyteller, offered a somewhat different ending:

I just want to tell you about what I heard when I was a little kid. My grandfather used to tell us stories about these stars and stuff like that, and that's the way I heard about this Big Dipper.

According to that story it was seven, but really it's eight. There was seven brothers, there was seven brothers, and they got one little sister, it's just one girl. And this little girl got a little puppy and she takes that puppy everywhere she goes. Wherever they go, that puppy went with them. So one day these seven brothers were kind of medicine men. Some of these medicine men, they don't want to be bothered by the other peoples, you know. One day, they were all sitting and talking.

One guy said, "Let's figure out something where we won't be bothered, where the people won't get near us." And one guy said, one brother said, "Well, let's try this one. The ash trees are the hardest woods there are." He says, "Why don't we go in the thick trees, thick woods and be ash trees and just stay right there. Maybe they don't bother us."

And one guy says, "That might be a good idea, but remember our grandmother used to gather wood and build a fire with it." He said, "Okay, that's right too."

Then one guy says, another brother said, "Let's try this way, it might work out. The rocks are hard, let's go up in the high mountains somewhere and be a rock and stay there. Maybe they don't bother us." Then again this man said, "That's right, too, but remember our grandmother used to break rocks and butcher with them." "Yep, that's right too."

Then one guy never say a word, just sat there thinking, "Why don't we try this way, this might be a good idea. Let's be Pipe Pointers." That means when the men smoke pipe, they usually point at these stars. That's when we're kind of wishing and kind of talk to them, stuff like that.

They said, "Okay, that's about the best idea. We'll go just as high as we can, stay right there, where the people can't reach us, don't bother us, and we be just right there. Maybe later some people smokes, smoke pipe and point at us and talk to us."

He said, "That's the best one," and he said, "I'll go first, and you'll follow me." And he point at one guy and said, "You take the last, tail end, and this little girl be in front of you. And you watch her, her and her puppy." He said, "Okay."

So they went up, they went up, one at a time. Next to the last comes the little girl, and then this other one's the last one, and watch this girl go up.

And one guy, the first one, the first one is this one here, [pointing at Polaris on a drawing of the constellations] and the second one is this one here [pointing at the star closest to Polaris in the bowl], the third one, and the fourth, fifth and the sixth one, and the seventh one. This one here, there used to be, I guess you noticed that there's a little bitty star by this one here. That's this girl with the puppy. And this is the last one. That's one I heard and I think that's a good one too.

Crow narratives exist in many versions, each one of which tells the same essential story. The primary message, the meaning and teaching of the story, stays the same, while embellishing details differ. These messages are important in the daily actions of the Crow people.

Chapter 7

THE SWEATLODGE AND THE STARS

THE CROW SWEATLODGE

The practices associated with the Crow sweatlodge are largely derived from the messages and lessons of the stars—the teachings of the sky. The rules and rites connected with the proper use of the sweatlodge are an integral part of Crow native beliefs. A simple dome-shaped structure made out of a framework of willows and covered with old blankets and tarps, with hot stones placed in a pit in the center or at the side of the lodge, can be seen as the core of contemporary native Crow beliefs. It is such an important aspect of native Crow philosophy that the use of one immediately categorizes the individual as one who follows the native ways of belief.

Once, when I was doing research on the history of the Pentecostal movement on the Crow Reservation, I gathered together a number of elderly couples who had knowledge of its beginnings. About six couples came to a friend's home and throughout the evening I queried them on the history of Pentecostalism on the reservation. As our discussions progressed I noticed that one man, a husband of one of the more vocal women, sat quietly and smoked hand-rolled cigarettes, the only smoker in the room. After a few hours I finally asked him directly what he knew of Crow Pentecostalism. They all laughed, and another man answered, "He doesn't know anything about it, the sweatlodge is his church."

This belief that the sweatlodge is central to Crow identity is brought out by the often-heard Crow concept that there are four things which make up the Crow: the Sacred Pipe, the clan system, the Tobacco Society, and the sweatlodge. The Sacred Pipe is seen as a symbol of leadership and peace, and the vehicle that conveys prayers; the clan system defines the individual's place within the social fabric of the Crow, with the mother's clan providing for the physical needs of the individual and the father's providing for the social recognition and religious needs; the Tobacco Society is the only religious organization that is specific to the Crow, and, in fact, is seen by Crow people as the ritual expression that differentiates them from all other nations. And, last is the sweatlodge, which provides for the physical and spiritual cleansing of the individual. Taken together, these four things are at the heart of what it means to be Crow.

The widespread respect that is accorded the sweatlodge comes through strongly in the well-known story of Big Metal. It tells of a boy who is thrown off a cliff by his stepfather and is rescued by seven sacred bighorn rams. Together with many other supernatural creatures, the Seven Rams give him very sacred powers. Because of the vast amount of power he is given, he is able to be disrespectful to people and supernatural beings. But, even with all this power he did not behave improperly to the sweatlodge. As the elder Lloyd expressed it:

> The sweat is the most sacred of all the ceremonies that we have, that's why it's stressed. In the story about Big Metal and the Seven Rams, it is said he was given all sorts of powers, by the birds and the animals that are about. He was so powerful, he was reckless, he would tease all the other sacred things, but not the sweat. He was instructed to never abuse the sweat. That's why the sacredness of the sweat is observed with a lot of respect and reverence, because of how this boy was instructed. The sweat is in relation to everything that is helpful, it's very helpful.

The ceremony of the sweatlodge also reinforces Crow concepts of the cycle of life, and of time in general. The Crow perceive time as cyclical, always repeating four stages: summer followed by fall, followed by winter, then spring, followed by summer again. The sweat ceremony, with its four "rounds," is said to mirror the four seasons of the year.

At the beginning of the first round, water is splashed on the heated rocks to represent the rain storms of the fall or spring, what

Crows call *xaláachke*, "the long rains." Termed *íihkupche*, this symbolic gesture represents the desire that all participating in the "sweat" may see those rains.

During each round a set number of ladles full of water is poured on the rocks: four, seven, ten, and finally the uncounted number, *chimmíssuua*, what Crows using English often call the "thousands" or "millions." To conclude each round, a participant must say a prayer to "raise the door." Usually these prayers are a recital of a sleep dream that predicts some coming season.

This is because the Crows firmly believe that dreams are predictive in nature. The events or seasons of the year that are seen in dreams are thought to be visions of things to come. They have three terms for dreams: dreams and visions in general are called *balewaashíale*; dreams which occur during sleep are called *balehámmaashiale*; and nightmares are termed *balewaashíalippiia*. Sleep dreams, sometimes spoken of as "wish dreams," are the ones utilized in the sweatlodge and whenever dream blessings are expected. Kirk, an elder from the Reno District, explained their importance:

> My dream last night would be *balewaashíale*. *Balewaashíale* means a dream or a vision. *Balehámmaashiale* means a sleep dream. We use them in everyday life. That's why when you go in the sweatlodge they'll say, "*Balehámmaashiale ítche koo iilíawaawuuk*" [Give to us good sleep dreams]. That means let us have good dreams.

> Dreams that pertain to the next season are used, like seeing green grass in my dream last night, then I could say, "I've seen springtime in my dream." If I was cutting somebody's cake or if someone gave me something at a giveaway, or in the sweatlodge, I could say, "I've seen this in my dreams, may we all go to that time," or in other words, we will all go, we will all see springtime in a good way, that's how that goes, that's how we use dreams.

> Even names, names that they hear in dreams, well naturally they'll name an infant or child that they were asked to name they'll use that name. So then, so with that dream then you are explaining with that dream, you are making a wish for that person. You are making a wish for somebody, proclaiming that you've seen the coming spring way ahead of time, to go to that time in a good way in between now and then. So that's how dreams are used.

> So for different ceremonial ways whatever it is, maybe a sweatlodge or cutting a birthday cake or giveaways as they pertain to a clan son or clan daughter, you are making a wish, a projection, projections for the future. The dream tellings are especially used around the sweatlodge.

Much more symbolism, beyond dreams, is included and incorporated into the sweatlodge. As an example, the Crow say that the world is composed of four elements: air, *huché*; earth, *awé*; water, *bilé*; and

fire, *bilée*. All four elements are present in the sweat: the air that carries the searing steam; the earth, our mother, that is sat upon; the
water that is poured on the hot rocks or drunk after the second
round; and the fire, the red hot rocks that have been heated in a fire.
To Carl these elements draw their power from the strongest forces in
nature:

> Let me make reference to something we believe in and discuss time
> and again. My children are particularly sensitive to this now because
> when they go to a ceremony, a worship ceremony, they hear us talking
> about this.
>
> When we offer prayer, offer a petition, or make a pleading, we acknowl-
> edge four things. First earth, call her Mother Earth, earth, fire, water,
> air. We acknowledge all four of them. When you put all that together,
> that's what we are; that's where we come from. We can't live without
> any one of them.
>
> So we use them in different ways, but we make that acknowledgment
> and that pleading to let us live in harmony. "Mother Earth, let us walk
> on your back for many many years. Fire, let us treat you with respect
> and you treat us kindly, warm and comfort us. Water, quench our
> thirst. Air, that we can use you to communicate when we need to."
>
> And of all the forces on earth, air is most precious, powerful, because
> without it I don't even get hungry, I die. I don't get thirsty, I die. So, in
> order, air, water, fire, and earth, we acknowledge them and want to
> live in harmony with them.
>
> We say that over and over again. "But we don't want to control you so
> treat us kindly," because when any one of those four begins to unleash
> its power, mankind has no power whatsoever, can't stand up to it.
>
> Wind storm comes, man with all his technology is powerless. Floods,
> man with all his technology can't stand up to it. Fire, when it takes off
> nothing can stand up in its path. Then this earthquake. They say when
> the earth moves, or the fire moves, or water moves, or wind moves,
> you're powerless.
>
> And my children are now coming back and saying, "Hey, that makes
> more sense now then ever." They said, "You don't know it, but it
> causes us to recall the prayers that have been described to us over and
> over and over again."

With all of this symbolic investment, the sweatlodge is also seen
as a personal cleansing, both physical and spiritual. As Lloyd discussed it when talking about the heroic Twins:

> We were talking about Thrown Into The Spring, and Thrown Behind
> The Lodge Lining. By the time the father gets them back, the one in the
> spring has forgotten that he's a human being, and they try to bring him
> back to his senses.

But nothing seems to work until he builds a sweat; the father, he puts on rawhide protectors on his arms, shoulders, and he takes his twin son in there and bodily immobilizes him and tells the other brother to keep pouring on, keep pouring it on until it gets real hot, just keep pouring.

So they go in there and the little guy doesn't know he's a human being, but they keep pouring water on the rocks, and it just gets hotter and hotter and hotter, until he screams "I'm burning, it's hot!" That's it, then he remembers that he's a human being.

So, here there's a sweat that has been handed down through the ages, that goes back to that story. Take a sweat, and remember or know who you are, know what you are, get back on track.

Usually the right to conduct a sweat ceremony, or "sweat rights," are passed from father to son. In most cases this is actually a classificatory father, what Crows call "clan fathers," or members of one's father's clan, since religious training and knowledge generally comes from individuals via this relationship. But the manner of performing a sweat is personally owned, since Crows generally consider religious rites to be personal property. A payment is made to recompense the individual for whatever they endured in order to gain the knowledge and right to perform the ceremony.

When inquiring about sweat ways, my own Crow family had me seek out one of my father's clan brothers who is known for his sweat rights. Through our lengthy discussion, I learned of the role of the stars in his "sweat way." Later, when he built a sweatlodge for me and my family and passed that way on to me, he concluded his instructions by saying, "Should anyone ask, you tell them your Papa gave this to you." I gave him four "good" physical gifts for his spiritual one.

This was the "star way" of conducting a sweat. Here the four pours of the first round represent the four seasons and four directions of the winds, the seven represent the Seven Brothers, or the Big Dipper, the ten represent the Gathering of Stars, the Pleiades, and the uncounted pours stand for all the stars in the sky.

In discussing his way to pour, he said there are four seasons, four directions of the wind. "Each wind means something else. A south wind means warmth, a west wind means a chinook, a north wind means cold is coming, an east wind means success, life, where light comes from, like that."

Then he explained the importance of the Seven Brothers, or *Ihka Sáhpua*, the Seven Stars: "They are brothers who are looking to help the Crow, that's why they are up there, they will last forever." He told me I should pray to them if I ever needed help, advice echoed by other elders.

As for the ten pours of the third round, "They are the ten closely set stars, *Ihkaxaxúa*." This term can be broken down into *ihké*, "stars" or "constellation" and *xaxúa*, "grouping" or "gathering." Thus, the Crow name of the Pleiades can be translated into English as "Gathering Of Stars." This particular "sweat way" appears to be the only place in which contemporary Crow people discuss the Pleiades. There are no elaborate stories about this constellation; when I asked, I was told it was simply a gathering of stars.

Since most observers usually see six or seven stars, sometimes nine, in this constellation, I asked my clan father if he knew where all ten were located and he said he did. He drew a picture of the ten stars of the Gathering Of Stars and also a line around them to represent the nebula of this constellation (see below).

The last round of ladles full of water he termed *Báakuku-taawaaakakoole*, "Where Above Ones Reside," which he had difficulty translating into English. At first he tried, "The atmosphere, the universe . . . ," but then turned to another elder present who said, "It's the stars, all the stars. They can't be counted." Others have defined this term to mean the cosmos in general, including the sun and moon, as well as the stars. Lastly, he advised me to look to the sky for the helpers, or providers of this way. If I should see them, I should raise my open hands to them, to greet them, to thank them for this way of life, this gift they have given humankind.

Albert, another elder who owns the star way, provided a slightly different explanation for the last "round" in this way. To him it was associated not only with the stars, but also with the abode of the deceased, for which he used the Crow term *kukéht asúuk*, "lodges on the other side." This term is often translated into English as the Other Side Camp, the Crow phrase for heaven.

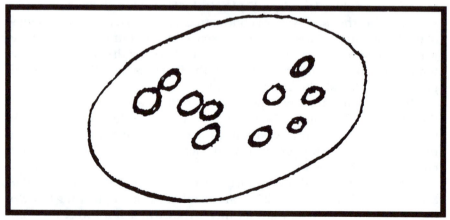

The Gathering Of Stars (Pleiades) as drawn by a Crow elder, 1994.

In the sweatlodge they pour water over the rocks four times, seven times, ten times, and then a million or uncounted times. The number four means the seasons: *báalee*, winter; *bíawukussee*, spring; *bíawakshe*, summer; *basée*, fall. It also means the first four poles of the sweatlodge structure. The first two poles, which make the doorway facing east, signify the arms of First Maker. The next two, which make up the back doorway, signify His legs. This means where they come in the front and go out in the back. Where the four poles come together in the center, where the hot rocks are placed and the water is poured, represents His body.

The seven pours of the second round represent the Pipe Pointer Stars, or the Seven Brothers I've mentioned. And the ten pours of the third time signify this *Ihkaxaxúa*, Gathering Of Stars.

And the last time is termed *chimmíssuua* [uncounted/infinite] or *dawússuua* [millions]. On a night when all of the stars light up, very bright, people say, "*Kukéht asúuk*" [lodges on the other side]. When people are facing death, they become afraid, and say things such as, "I am afraid to die, I don't want to die." They are told, "Don't be afraid, even if you die you will be alive up there." This is what the term "*Kukéht asúuk*" means.

People of many generations ago that have died, have moved camp and are all together, well and happy. They were here with us, but now they are gathered up there. There are many of them. Some have gone up there and they were told to come back because their time was not yet.

That is how we know of these things. We are told of them by people that have been there and back. This is how we speak of the term heaven. This is the significance of the term, "*Kukéht asúuk*."

THE SEVEN BUFFALO BULLS

To many Crow people the origin of the sweatlodge is associated with a variant of the Big Dipper story that features the Sacred Seven Buffalo Bulls. Kirk, an elder from the Reno District, talked about their names, and how they are associated with the sweatlodge and the Big Dipper:

The Seven Buffalo Bulls are mentioned a lot of times when we go in the sweatlodges. Those seven are called, wait—their leader is *Chíilapbaa-laaxaachish*, Crazy Bull, then there is *Chíilapish* [The Bull], *Aashi-isássaash* [Horns Turned Forward], and *Iaxaapahúsh* [Thin Hair Places On The Hide], and *Chíilapaakkeekoohuush*, [Bull Who Reaches

The Near Bank], and *Chíilabaaalaxaiileetash* [Brave Bull], and *Chíilapkalishtachiash* [Young White Buffalo]. Those are the ones they mainly use in the sweatlodge.

That is where they point the peace pipe too, up there. You have probably heard that—*Iipchalapaachuoo* [Pipe Pointer Stars]. Both are the Big Dipper. That's why some individuals when they build a new sweat they will use a peace pipe in there and when they get through smoking, they put the peace pipe on top of the sweatlodge. Only when a new sweatlodge is built have I seen that.

Generally the Crow think of these Seven Buffalo Bulls as representing brotherly love and as a model of how people should ideally work together. They are described as taking turns leading the herd to new places and always helping each other. The following story describes how the Big Dipper became associated with the sweatlodge through the adoption of an abandoned human boy by the Seven Sacred Buffalo Bulls. In this version there is also a reference to a native Crow women's game called *búupchalapiio*, "kicking the ball." Most often played individually, it could also be played in a group. When the game was played by a single person, the object was to keep the ball in the air as long as possible. In a group, the object was to keep the ball in the air by kicking from person to person, much like the game presently fashionable among college students called hacky sack.

Also in this version, we hear a common Crow expression that underscores the importance of children to the Crow people, even when it is an adopted child. For when the boy adopted by the Seven Buffalo Bulls is threatened by the villainous *Hummachiish*, the Bulls come to the boy's aid, "For the love of their little child." This expression, *daláakichisshiiwaashcheek*, "For the love of your child," is used as a plea which cannot be denied.

This version of the Seven Buffalo Bulls story was provided by Oscar, an elder from the Big Horn District:

One of the stories that is still talked about today, that relates to the sweatlodge, is the Seven Buffalo Bulls. There was a girl who was a daughter of a chief. Her father refused all the young men who asked to marry her. However, she became pregnant. When her condition began to show, she tried to hide it but she knew that it would only get worse. When the time came for her to have the baby, the camp was moving. She told her father that she had a stomachache and wanted to rest. She rode off to a buffalo wallow and there had the child.

There were Seven Buffalo Bulls that were out wandering around and they noticed an object out on the prairie. They thought it was an animal. They went close to it and found it was a human baby. They retrieved this little child, it was a little boy. Their leader was named *Chíilapbaalaaxaachish* [Crazy Bull]. Crazy Bull came and horned the baby into the air. The first time the boy landed he could crawl around, the second time he was a toddler, the third time he could walk and speak. And when Crazy Bull threw the boy in the air the fourth time, the boy landed on his feet and he was a teenager.

These Seven Buffalo Bulls raised their little son. They named him *Bishéeshikaakash*, Buffalo Boy. Crazy Bull was very fond of his son, he would provide the boy with things to eat. As the boy matured, he became a good-looking man.

There was a tyrannical bull named *Hummachiish* [Bones Together], "The Bull With The Connecting Bones." It was impossible to injure or destroy him because his bones were all connected together on the outside of his body. The only opening was on his rump and his *alaakáwe* [the soft area above the collarbone].

He had two wives and he was very jealous of his younger wife. The Seven Buffalo Bulls instructed the boy not to take any water that was offered to him from this young woman. By chance their paths crossed and this young woman offered Buffalo Boy some water and Buffalo Boy said, "Nope, my brothers told me not to drink your water." This woman touched her hand to the water and put it on his lips and said, "You drank my water anyway." She went and told her husband. Her husband was furious and he called on this boy.

For the love of their little child the Seven Buffalo Bulls stood up to *Hummachiish*, the buffalo bull that had bones that were solid. And one by one *Hummachiish* defeated these buffalo bulls. He broke their legs and crippled them. Finally he said, "Buffalo Boy, you are next."

Buffalo Boy came out of a tipi and he had an eagle plume tucked behind on his head. *Hummachiish* was wallowing and pawing up the ground. He was throwing up the dust and rubbing up his horns on the ground and he charged Buffalo Boy. Buffalo Boy jumped up in the air and the buffalo ran under him. The boy turned around in the air and shot an arrow into the rump of the bull. *Hummachiish* then went and rubbed his horns on the ground and pawed the ground and he charged Buffalo Boy again. This time the boy shot him in the collar. Blood oozed out his nostrils and he died. The buffalo that had been in *Hummachiish*'s herd ran off because they did not know that humans had that much power. So then Buffalo Boy took his brothers into a sweatlodge and when they came out they were all well, their broken bones were mended and they were all well.

The buffalo became afraid of this young man and the Crows were having a tough time, so the Bulls decided that it was time to send their child home. They instructed him and they advised him. Crazy Bull gave him a bag of kidney fat and instructed him that when the moon was near to the horizon, he could use this to make the buffalo come near. He told his son, "As you approach camp, there will be girls playing *búupchalapiio* [kicking the ball], and as you approach them, lie down and a ball will come rolling to you. You grab the ball and hold on to it. A good-looking young woman will walk up to you and ask you for her ball. She will say, 'Young man, give me my ball,' and that will be your mother, call her mother."

The boy did as he was instructed when he got home. He walked into camp and there was these women playing the ball game. He walked up there and he sat down. He did as he was instructed. He was laying on the ground with his hand on his chin when this ball rolled to him and he picked it up and held onto it. Then this young lady came up to him and said to him, "Young man, give me my ball." And he said, "Mother!" And she said, "Why am I your mother?" She cried and took off and ran to her father. This boy went to the chief's lodge and the chief asked, "Why did you call my daughter your mother?" The boy said, "You kept abusing my mother until she got pregnant, and when I was born she left me on the trail to die. Some buffalos took me in and raised me and that is why I called her mother."

Then this boy walked out of the lodge and he was never seen after that. They say that he went to the sky and became the North Star and his fathers are the Big Dipper. They took their little son and he became the North Star. That is one of the sources of the sweatlodge.

The Seven Buffalo Bulls are therefore also thought to dwell in the Big Dipper. They are believed to occasionally come down from the heavens and make their presence known in the sweatlodge. Albert, an elder from the Wyola District, stated:

> The Big Dipper is also called the Seven Bulls. When they have special sweats the spirits of these Bulls come, I am told. When they have the sweat and the Seven Bulls come, they would know when they would come, you know. As the men lay around the sweat, the older ones believe and know of them, so they would say "These are the Seven Bulls."
>
> When the Bulls come into a sweat like that, we are told it is very great and powerful. The Seven Bulls relate to the sweatlodge. Yes, the Seven Bulls, I know of how they come down at times when people hold a sweat. They know when they come. The people, as they lay around in the sweatlodge, they could tell. They could feel the presence of the Bulls. They would say, "The Seven Bulls are here." I guess they would also snort. They would say, "It's good!, It's good! The Seven Bulls are here."

Besides providing one form of sweat way to the Crow, the Seven Buffalo Bulls also are believed to have brought the Sacred Arrows and the Sacred Pipes to the Crow. The first Sacred Pipe was brought to the Crow by a woman who had been adopted by the Seven Bulls. Because of her association with these beings, she has become known as *Bishéewiash*, "Buffalo Woman," just as the boy who was adopted before her has been called *Bishéeshikaakash*, "Buffalo Boy." Peter, an elder from Pryor, provided the detailed and extensive story of how this woman came to be associated with the Seven Bulls, and how they came to give the first Sacred Arrow to the Crow. This story also describes the relationship of the Seven Brothers to the Seven Bulls. Another elder jokingly referred to this variant of the Seven Bulls story as the Crow version of *Snow White and the Seven Dwarfs*:

> This story is about the *Chíilapsahpuua* [the Seven Bulls] in Crow. As the story goes, they turned themselves into people. This is a very old story, from a long time ago. There are still things around that we hear of, such as *Hisshishtawia* [Red Woman], and beings in the water that eat people.

> In olden days the Crows would move about, and on these occasions when they moved, a young virtuous woman would disappear. No one would hear of them any more. This happened until the people began to be curious. They searched among themselves and asked about the women that kept disappearing. They went from one person to another until one man said, "Wait. Let me alone with this for awhile and I will tell you what I find." Up to this point many men had used their powers to find out what was happening to these women, but no one could come up with the answer.

> Now this one man, after he meditated for awhile, said, "It's *Iisbishéet-bishish* [Worms In His Face] that's been doing this to you. He is a very handsome man. At a certain time he goes out looking for women, but I don't know much more after that. This is all I know for now."

> There was a virtuous woman who was very beautiful. Men would give her gifts and try to go out with her and she would refuse each one. Her mother told her, "You had better marry one of these men." But the girl told her, "No." Her grandmother said, "I don't know what she is waiting for, maybe *Iisbishéetbishish*."

> All types of men asked her to marry them and she refused every one of them and then one night this virtuous woman was getting ready to go to bed, so she went out to use the bathroom. This man came up to her and she could see that he was a very handsome man and had an aroma of fine perfume. He said, "I came to see you. I want to ask you out." This woman looked this man over and he was very good looking. She told him, "I will go in and get dressed and I will be back out." She came out and the young man asked her if she was ready to go and the young woman told him, "Yes." So they went. She went following him as he took the lead.

They went until it was daybreak. They would rest awhile and then go and as they got tired, then they would rest again, and then go again. They went on until it got dark. They stopped and slept. Each in their own bedroll. They got up in the morning and started out again.

A bird, a snowbird, came to this woman and told her, "*Iisbishéetbishish* is the one that is taking you. It will take four days to reach his home. On the third night then he will take you to bed. When he does, in the morning worms will be all over his face. When he gets a hold of a young virtuous lady, they would see his face, get frightened and run away. He would catch up to them as they run away, kill them and give them to his parents to eat. Too, I want to tell you that when you see all the worms on his face then put your face right up to his face and that will solve the matter, no more worms."

Just as the bird had said, on the morning after the third night, she woke and saw his face decayed and covered with worms. She put her face right up to the face of *Iisbishéetbishish*, the young lady rubbed his cheeks with her cheeks, and the young man was good to look at again. Sure enough, as he woke up he saw his face and he was one handsome man. The woman was not afraid and he was happy.

They got up, got ready, and started out again. They went until they got to a place where there was a river. On the other side of the river was a camp. It belonged to this young man's grandmother. As they got to the camp, the young lady noticed that *Iisbishéetbishish* was living with his grandmother. They stayed there.

The grandmother felt sorry for the young lady because she knew what was going to happen to her. The next day the grandmother told the young lady to go to the brush, there was someone there that wanted to see her. So she went on her way and met a man there, who was really a mouse.

This mouse told her, "This man *Iisbishéetbishish* brings women to his camp and then when he tires of them he gives them over to his parents. His parents are water reptiles and they would eat them for their meal." He told her, "Make a buckskin dress and a new pair of moccasins. Make the moccasin strings long enough so that they drag behind you a little bit. This will be good." As she went off, the mouse said, "He will try to go to his folks with you in the morning. There is a rotted buffalo skull that he will ask you to stand on. Tomorrow will be the day that he will try to take you, for his folks to eat you."

The next morning *Iisbishéetbishish* got the woman up and told her they were going to the river to bathe. But the grandmother knew his plans were to feed her to his parents so she said, "Wait, let us see if she can make some buckskin." The man said it was okay and the grandmother gave the young lady a rawhide and told her to go over to the hills to make some buckskin. She went off to make buckskin.

She came upon some very large ants. She cried to the ants, "I am in this predicament. *Iisbishéetbishish* wants to feed me to his parents. If they are going to eat me, then I have no say. Look upon me and see if you can help me, for I have to make this buckskin." They told her to put the hide on the top of their house. She did as they said. By the time the ants got through with the hide, it was one of the best, and most beautiful buckskin hides that anyone had ever seen.

After the buckskin was finished, she took it and started to make herself a dress. The mouse had told her to make good stitches on the dress and make it so that it would not come off, and with the moccasins too. He had said, "Make the moccasin strings long, even dragging a little if you have to."

The next morning the man woke up the young lady and told her they were going to bathe. She knew his plans and dressed in her new buckskin outfit and moccasins. The grandmother said to her, "Young lady, this is the time the person told you about, when he will give you to his parents to eat. Plead with him, do your best to talk him out of it. I started my boiling pot early this morning. If you get away from him, when you come it will be at its hottest. When you come, get my axe and cut me up into pieces and throw me into the pot. Take my arm and axe and put it in the woods. If you do this and put me there carrying my axe, then I can be of help to you."

They started out. They went until they got to the place where they were to take a bath and she checked out the place. The mouse was there. This person told her, "When you stand on the skull we will hold the strings on your moccasin so he can't push you in." *Iisbishéetbishish* said, "Okay, let's go swimming." The man asked her, "How come you have a nice dress to go swimming?" She replied, "I have just finished this, that's why I am wearing it. I want to wear it after I get out of the water."

He asked the lady to step up on the rotted buffalo skull, he also got on it and tried the water. He watched, he was wary for his parents. He bent down and drank some water quietly. He was very alert, he was looking for his parents. As he stood above the water, the man called, "Father, here is your meal." But as he was going to throw her over, the little people grabbed on to the strings on her moccasins, and *Iisbishéetbishish* slipped and fell in. His parents were *bulúksee* [large flesh-eating reptile] and they ate him. Fighting over him they didn't know that it was him.

The young lady ran back to the grandmother. The grandmother told the young lady, "Get his perfume, mirror, rouge, and comb. It might be helpful for your escape." In the olden days the comb was sacred for they used it as medicine. The perfume was made of snowberry and pine needles. It was used with the comb. She took this. The mirror was a square stone. They would rub it over and over until it was to the point where you could see yourself. The fourth thing was his rouge, his face paint.

The grandmother said, "Now get going. As you go along, when he about overtakes you, throw one of these things you are carrying behind you. Way over in the mountains, where there are no clouds, there is a white tipi there. If you manage to make it to the mountain and to the house, those who live there might be able to help you. Call out, 'Iiwakkuluu, Iisbishéetbishish is trying to kill me.' If you say this he will help you."

She got things together, chopped up this grandmother as she had instructed her to do. She picked up the pieces of this old lady and put her into the boiling pot, took her arm and axe, went into the forest and left it there. She began to run away.

Back in the water the bulúksee had eaten their child. Suddenly the parents recognized his bracelet. The parents in the water said, "We did a bad thing. We ate our son." So they vomited him back up. Then they started to blame each other [laughs]. Then they gathered together the pieces of Iisbishéetbishish and almost finished, but they couldn't find one of his eyes. They put in the other eye and he was able to see. He stumbled about. He went back to his grandmother's camp. He called out, "Grandmother! Grandmother! Where are you?" His grandmother replied, "Here I am. Wait a minute." He replied, "You have to hurry. The young lady, I don't know where she went." He tried to hurry her, but she didn't come, he could hear her chopping wood. Iisbishéetbish-ish got angry with her and said, "What kind of a grandmother are you anyway. I'm in a hurry. What are you doing that should take time like this?" He followed the sound of the chopping and when he reached there he saw just her arm was there. "Oh my! She's done it to me now."

Iisbishéetbishish thought that she went out toward the mountains, so he started out toward the mountain. Soon he saw the young lady in the distance. He yelled, "Stop! You caused me and my grandmother to be killed. You got the best of us. But as it turns out, you will be eaten anyway so you may as well not run any further."

He was starting to catch up to her. So she threw his mirror behind her. As the mirror struck the ground, big ravines appeared. Iisbishéetbish-ish fell into one. Ravines are where the earth is cracked up and is opened. Some are very large and deep. There are some so deep that when a person gets into one he can't get out so he stays in there until he dies.

But Iisbishéetbishish crawled out and as he was catching up to her, he warned her again, "Don't go any further. You will be eaten anyway." She got the perfume and threw it. There was a body of water between them. It was very large. The man then took a piece of wood and used it as a float to cross the water. He again came close to her. She turned and threw the hair comb. Where she threw the comb, there was so much cactus all over he had trouble getting over it. As he started to catch up to her again, she threw his rouge and it spread over the land as a cloud. He said, "This woman has gotten the best of me." He was forced to stop and pick up the rouge piece by piece until he picked it all up.

She ran up toward the mountain until she came to the tipi that she was told about. She called out, "*Iiwakkuluu*, help me. *Iisbishéetbishish* is chasing me and I need your help." A voice called from inside, "Go around the house four times and then come in." The tipi was made of stone and had only one door. As she went the fourth time, the door was opened for her.

Just then *Iisbishéetbishish* saw what had happened and called out, "*Iiwakkuluu*, give me back the woman. My parents want to eat her." *Iiwakkuluuush* replied, "She has come into my house and you can't do anything now. I will not give her back to you. You must not be as much of a man as you think."

This *Iiwakkuluuush* had seven brothers who were away from the tipi and had not come back yet. They were the Seven Bulls. They would turn themselves into men and go out to work and come back in the evening. They would chop wood and do other chores. *Iiwakkuluuush* stayed home to watch it. He loved to eat and he was very fat. He is the greatest of the brothers. Each brother had different abilities. One had great upper body strength, one was a great runner, one had much knowledge, one had great stamina, one had strong legs, and one had great memory. But *Iiwakkuluuush* was the most religious one. He has a lot of power.

Iisbishéetbishish called out, "If you are half the man that you think you are come out and fight me." *Iiwakkuluuush* replied, "You will have to win. You will have to kill me. That is the only way that you can get her back. You will have to kill me." They argued like that until finally *Iiwakkuluuush* went outside and they went at it. Oh, did they ever fight. They were going at it strong, when the brothers came home.

The brothers got *Iisbishéetbishish* and tied him up good. They gathered a bunch of wood and piled it on him and burned him up. In the midst of the fire they could hear him pleading to be set free. They put back any ember that popped out of the fire to make sure everything was burned up. They all kept watch of the fire, not allowing anything out of the fire. He quit talking and they had thought that all of him had burnt up, so they put out the fire and said amongst themselves that there will never more be anything like *Iisbishéetbishish*.

As they were returning home, *Iiwakkuluuush* asked, "Hey, brothers, do you love me?" They answered, "Yes." He asked them over and over again. Finally the others asked, "Why do you keep asking us this over and over?" He replied, "I have a little sister." They were surprised. "You have no sister," they said. He spoke, "*Iisbishéetbishish* chased a young woman my way, so I had her hide in my house so now I have a little sister. I took her for my sister."

One of the brothers said to *Iiwakkuluush*, "You don't even know how to have a sister, give her to me and I will marry her." *Iiwakkuluush* got upset and started to cry. The others got after this brother and told him to leave *Iiwakkuluush* alone. And they all accepted the young lady as their sister.

Time passed and they all continued to live together as a family. They went on to live their lives. Every day they would go out to work and even *Iiwakkuluush* would go along with the others and leave the sister home to do the household chores. She would have their supper all ready by the time they came home. They would eat, and she would clean up after them and was a very efficient woman. The brothers were pleased to have her as a sister. They loved their sister very dearly.

One day the sister heard a voice, it sounded like it was singing, but she couldn't make out very well what was said. It came closer, and closer and became clearer. She remembered in times past that *Iiwakkuluush* had told her not to let anyone in the tipi if she was alone. It was Red Woman singing a lullaby to her baby that was a little screech owl. The words were, "I wonder how I can eat *Iiwakkuluush*'s kidney, don't you cry."

She got to the house and asked the young lady inside, "Let me in and we can have a good sweat together." She refused to answer her, so the Red Woman walked around the house until she found a broken stone, out of place. "Ah! this is the door," she said. She went inside. The young lady was surprised and of course she was in a helpless situation, so she fed Red Woman. Red Woman would stay until she would hear the brothers coming home. The young lady would want to tell the brothers about Red Woman, but she would forget. This went on for quite some time.

One day Red Woman came as usual, singing her lullaby to her baby. She came in at the cracked place in the stone wall. The sister was picking up things, and on the floor she saw a feather. She thought to herself, "I will keep this to remember Red Woman's visit by." So she stuck the feather in her hair. Red Woman hung around, ate, and everything she usually did and then left.

That night, *Iiwakkuluush* saw the feather in his sister's hair and asked her, "Sister, what is the feather you have in your hair?" She took the feather out of her hair and remembered. She told her brother, "It is like this, Red Woman would come every day and sing a song. The song said, 'How can I eat *Iiwakkuluush*'s kidney' and I would want to tell you but I would forget every time." The brother said, "It is true. This woman is treacherous. She has medicine is the reason that you can't remember to tell me. She causes you to forget. I am glad you told me."

He asked the brothers, "What shall we do about this?" They all gathered around and discussed how they could put an end to Red Woman. The one that was knowledgeable said, "Let's catch her and we'll put an end to her treacherous ways so that there will not be one like her again." Another asked, "How can we do that?" The sister said, "She always wants to go in a sweat, maybe we can catch her that way." The brothers said, "Good. That's what we will do."

So, they got the sweatlodge ready, they got a lot of wood, and waited. They told the sister, "When she comes, we will hide around the sweat. Just hope that she does not see us. Get her inside and call out to us so we know that you have her. Then we will come in and get her. This is the only way we can get her. This is the only way we can get her and destroy her works. Otherwise, she will do much harm to our people in the future."

About the time that the brothers usually left the home, Red Woman came, singing her song. *Iiwakkuluush* said, "Here she comes. Hide!" So they hid and kept real still and quiet. She got to the house and sensed something was up. She looked around the house and thought, "It smells like *Iiwakkuluush*." She looked around, but didn't see anything, so she thought, "Oh well, I guess I am wrong." So she went in the house through the crack. She announced her coming to the young lady. The young lady fed her as usual. She kept singing to the baby owl, "How can I eat *Iiwakkuluush*'s kidney?"

The young lady jumped on her and put her arm around Red Woman's neck and called out, "Come! Hurry! I've got her." They all came and got her and tied her up to where she could not move. One had the sweat already burning with hot rocks. She told them, "Let me go, or I will kill all of you. You have no charm or anything to do away with me. Let me go." *Iiwakkuluush* said, "No. We don't like the way you have been treating people, so we are going to do away with you."

As they got into the sweat, Red Woman took something from the ground and put it around the top of her head. *Iiwakkuluush* poured on the water and made it real hot. But Red Woman said, "Keep the water coming." As the sweat started, the seven brothers changed themselves into buffalo bulls. They snorted like buffalo. *Iiwakkuluush* poured the water on over, over, and over, until it got very hot. Red Woman kept singing and singing away.

Then *Iiwakkuluush* and Red Woman matched their medicine. Red Woman would shoot light from her eyes as lightning. *Iiwakkuluush* would snort like a buffalo and send forth his medicine. He kept on, saying he wanted to destroy her. He said, "I will bring you to nothing." Red Woman was getting weaker, but she still said, "I will kill all seven of you." *Iiwakkuluush* wouldn't quit. The others were getting weaker though. She still said, "I am stronger than you. I will still get the best of you." *Iiwakkuluush* kept on until she got very weak. Soon the lightning of her eyes gave out. She was getting uncoordinated and she was out of her mind. She fell to the ground, cowering. *Iiwakkuluush* quit pouring water over the rocks.

Red Woman said, "*Iiwakkuluu* you have gotten the best of me. Open the door and let me out." *Iiwakkuluush* said, "No!" And he poured more water on the rocks. She cried out, "You're burning me now, let me go." He put on more and more water until Red Woman was really burning up. She screamed in pain, but he kept putting on more water. She began pleading with him to let her go but it was no use, he wouldn't listen. She was asking and begging until her speech was slurred, and she was in so much pain that she kept rolling and rolling, mumbling and mumbling. Soon she couldn't even talk anymore of anything. *Iiwakkuluush* stopped pouring.

He said, "I have done you in." He opened the door and told her to leave. He said, "You will never be like you were again. You have no powers anymore to make others do what you want. You go out and live like the rest of us, work at getting food to eat and work at making a living. Go!" She went, looking all defeated and kept on going till she was out of sight.

Then these brothers and their sister continued on, until one day *Iiwakkuluush* said, "Think, if one day she returns and seeks revenge, it will be devastating. She could wipe us out. We should think of something to do. Let's become something that is eternal, that can never be destroyed." One said, "How about water in a river?" *Iiwakkuluush* said, "No, water evaporates." Another said, "What about stones?" *Iiwakkuluush* answered, "No, they break into pieces." "Trees?" another said. "No, trees get old, fall, and rot away and sometimes they chop them for fire wood," replied *Iiwakkuluush*. Then another suggested, "How about mountains?" "No," said *Iiwakkuluush*, "They have volcanoes, they erupt, they have fire, and burn up, think of something else."

Finally they ran out of ideas and they asked the one that was knowledgeable, "Look upon us and help us out." He sat thinking for a long time and said, "Tonight as you go outside, you see the skies and they are all lit with the stars. From the day that I can remember, they have always been there. Let us become stars. We will stay close together and on a day that our people go through hard times and need help, they can offer us tobacco and we can help our people."

After all agreed on this, *Iiwakkuluush* spoke up, "Can I take my sister?" The knowledgeable one said, "No, she has her own people and she can return to them." They led her close to her people and told her the direction to go. They told her, "As you go along the way, four babies will come up to meet you. Don't pick them up. Leave them alone. Just keep on going."

So she went. She came upon a little baby, but she passed him by and continued on her trip. She again came up on another little baby, but passed that one up too. Also a third one, she passed this one up too. The brothers were watching her from the heavens and said, "She has one left. I hope she doesn't pick that one up." She went on until it got dark. She slept, and in the morning she started out again. She met the fourth little baby. The baby was just starting to walk. It was staggering, falling, getting up and trying again, and she hit her nose in a fall and it bled. The young lady picked her up and wiped the blood off her face, packed her and went on with her. The brothers were very displeased with the young lady. They said she had not followed instructions.

This young lady went on, her name was *Bishéewiash* [Buffalo Woman]. The people rejoiced as this young lady returned. She had been gone so long, but now she had returned. They were amazed to see her and she had come home with a child.

That night the little one cried all night until dawn. No one could do anything to stop her crying. At the time that night got to the darkest, the dark face time, she all of a sudden quit crying. This child's name was One That Cuts Out A Heart. As the people got into a deep sleep, the baby flew out of the smoke hole. She flew from tipi to tipi looking into the smoke hole. She looked everyone over and went into a chief's tipi. She stood over him, looking at him, and then quickly, she took out the chief's heart. She flew over to a tree, sat under it, and ate up the heart. In the morning, when the chief was discovered, the people were screaming and crying.

This kept happening, but only to brave men. Only the hearts of warriors and pipe carriers were eaten by this baby. The people began to wonder. They began to go among all of the men. They asked them if they knew, but no one could help. No one could help until they came up to a young man who said he would fast in the mountains and see if he could find out what was doing this. He went to the mountains and fasted and there he had a vision of the Seven Bulls. They gave him a Sacred Arrow and they told him, "With this you can find the treacherous one."

He returned to his camp and told the people of his vision. He had the arrow as his medicine. He said, "At night cover the door, and don't go outside." He brought the arrow and stood it in the middle of the tipi. They covered the door, the arrow was in place in the middle of the tipi. The arrow would find and kill the treacherous one. Nothing happened for several days. He told the people not to touch the arrow. In the olden days, when people were instructed not to touch the medicine, they would not touch it.

The people began to watch the arrow. Then came time when this child began to play sick. She cried and cried all night. It came the time just before morning when it is pitch dark. Now, when dark face time would come, all would go to sleep. Then this child would come out into the open. She knew about the arrow, so she was watching it. She went real fast and went to the home of another old warrior. She flew in and ate the man's heart, and flew back to her home and went to bed.

Now, the arrow owner knew who it was. He went to the woman and said, "It is your child. Why didn't you tell us?" She denied it and pointed to the baby sleeping. But the other men came and she cried, "It is not my baby. One morning I picked her up and she had a piece of meat in her teeth. It was a piece of a human heart!"

Then the men jumped on the baby to kill it, but she woke up and started singing, "My body is impenetrable, arrows cannot hurt me." She kept jumping from man to man, landing at each man's feet. She kept singing and jumping. A man said, "Go get the arrow man and ask for his help." This man came and said, "She is too powerful and dangerous, but I'll do what I can." The man brought the arrow and made medicine. He shot the arrow and killed the baby. This is the story of the Seven Bulls.

The previous narrative relates much more than how Buffalo Woman came to be adopted by the Seven Buffalo Bulls, it also shows the drawbacks of vanity, the importance of following the instructions of the supernatural, and the use of the sweatlodge to overcome evil. Another narrative tells how Crow people received the first Sacred Pipe from the Seven Buffalo Bulls through their daughter, Buffalo Woman. Lloyd, an elder from the Black Lodge District, provided a brief version of this narrative:

The Sacred Pipe comes from the Big Dipper—the Seven Sacred Buffalo Bulls as we say. The story behind that is there were two men out hunting deer. When they went to rest along the river, one of them saw a light coming at them in the sky.

This man told his partner, but the other one thought it was a trick and wouldn't look up. His friend made him look and they both saw a beautiful woman in a pure white buckskin dress carrying a Sacred Pipe in her arms.

She gave these two the pipe. It was a gift from the Big Dipper brought by their daughter *Bishéewiash* [Buffalo Woman].

Albert, the Crow elder who owns the only functioning Sacred Pipe among the Crow today, explained to me the significance of the Sacred Pipe, the meanings of its decoration, and how it is used:

I have a Sacred Pipe. I am probably the only one that has this today. Many Crows used to have one. I want to talk about these Sacred Pipes now. I take it out at certain times. I haven't taken it out for several summers now. The story I told you of the Seven Bulls—the Big Dipper, this is where the Medicine Pipe comes from.

On the end of the pipestem is a mallard's head. You know where the head of a mallard is blue, that is what is on the pipestem. The reason they use the mallard head is because of its significance at the time of creation, I was told. There was no land here before. It is said that there was nothing but water everywhere, so *Iichíhkbaalee* [First Maker] called four mallards. He told them, "I want to make land, dive into the water, and get me some mud. I will make dry land with that." One of the mallards went into the water but came up with nothing. The next one was the same, and so was the next one. Then the fourth one went into the water. He was gone for a long time and *Iichíhkbaalee* thought that the mallard had died, but then He saw the mallard coming with mud in his beak.

He took the mud and made the earth as we know it today. He moved portions of water that today are the oceans, lakes, and rivers. He molded the mountains, hills, valleys, and so forth. He made man also. He breathed into the first people, giving them life and speech. He made people of all nations, but the Crows He made first and told them that they would be the closest to Him. He told them that He would be with them and He made everything for them. The head of the mallard that I told you about, that is on the end of the pipestem. It is said that this mallard is the one that found land, and, therefore, he is to be up on the end of the stem of the Medicine Pipe.

The other decorations are blue beads on the stem, they represent the sky. There are owl feathers on the end from the Great Horned Owl which represents his power, his good messages. There are eagle plumes which represents the dog, the protector of man. Then there is red and white horse hair, the red horse hair represents the clouds seen at sunset, the white represents the clouds that bring rain. And last, there are seven eagle feathers that are tied together and put on the pipestem. They hang down like a fan. These feathers represent the Seven Bulls.

There is an occasion that is called Dancing To The Sacred Pipe. I have seen this happen twice in my lifetime. It was when I was young. They opened the Sacred Pipe Bundle and they danced to it. They carried rattles and danced towards the pipes. They sang four songs.

There is an adoption that goes along with the Sacred Pipe. A person can make a vow, such as, "If we dwell safely through the next year, I will open the Sacred Pipe Bundle." If the vow comes true then they pay to be adopted into the Sacred Pipe Society. They prepare food and a Sacred Pipe owner adopts them. This is a way of life, too.

There are many songs for these ceremonies. It is a singer that is hard to find. He would sing four of the songs, then on the last one, he would sing, "I am going to eat." Then a person would pray; then they would eat. That's the way it is done. This Sacred Pipe came from the Seven Bulls, as we are told. We are told not to let the Sacred Pipe touch the ground. It came from above, so we are told not to let it touch the earth. The times it is opened, they would spread out a cloth first, before they put the Sacred Pipe down. These are the rules for the Sacred Pipe. So, the Sacred Pipe comes from the Big Dipper. That is what I know of the things that go with the Sacred Pipes.

The star beings have invested and provided their power to the Crow people in a number of different ways. The sweatlodge, the Sacred Arrows, the Sacred Pipe, and many other gifts from the stars have given the Crow a means of survival—a way of life.

Chapter 8

MOVING LIGHTS
OF THE NIGHT

COMETS, METEORS, AND SHOOTING STARS

When a comet streaked across the sky the Crows would often see it as a portent of a coming battle or of the impending death of someone important to the tribe. Ironically, the negative qualities attributed to comets by the old-time Crow were only reinforced by their exposure to Christianity. As they came to call the devil *chiishbishe*, "has a tail," some Crow elders would translate the name for comet, *ihkachiishpishe*, "star with a tail," as the "Devil Star."

The comet most widely remembered by contemporary Crow elders is the appearance of Halley's Comet in the spring of 1910. Carl explained the origin of the name for comets with reference to that event:

Halley's Comet is the one that they called *Ihkachiishpishe* [Star With A Tail], it may be other comets too, but that's the one that gained the notoriety, they remembered seeing it, and it was dangerous, it could've ended our lives. When it came in the early 1900s, I remember stories where they said it could bring the end of life as we know it, it could've been. They say when they're ready to die they put on things they want to be put to rest with. They'd put those on and go to bed, thinking they may not live through the night, because of that comet.

Carl went on to explain that the old men of the St. Xavier community stayed awake the whole time that Halley's Comet was visible. Dressed in their best clothes, they gathered at the community's meeting hall and sang songs all night long. Because of the comet, they feared that each night might be their last. So they wanted to be well dressed and with friends singing joyous songs. Albert remembered how his father never forgot this frightening time:

The Star With A Tail, yes, they say that the Star With A Tail goes by every so many years. When they knew when it was going to come, not knowing what it was, the elders put on their best apparel and waited anxiously. When it came, it would go by throwing off sparks, all lit up, catching attention. It comes only every so often. I think it had some stars forming a tail-like thing that was seen, this is why it is called the Star With A Tail. I guess it was considered phenomenal. The star would come and behind it would come the tail that threw off sparkling lights. It was a real long tail, I was told.

My father said they all saw it and it was really something. They thought that something was going to happen and everyone was afraid. It comes every so many years. I for myself have never seen it, but the generation before me saw it. The elders saw it. They had their good apparel on for this occasion. They thought that something was going to happen to them and that is the reason for their dress.

When it came they marveled at the greatness of this star. Its tail was glittering so much, it threw sparks all over as it went. It was so bright and lit the earth. They couldn't explain it and it was something they could not understand, therefore they were afraid of it. They thought that it would take them, or kill them off, they didn't know. I am about 81 and I never saw it. The ones that saw it were the ones before me. That's quite a long while ago, isn't it?

Hanna, an elder from Ft. Smith, described how the community reacted to the sighting of a comet:

I will tell you of the comet. They knew the comet, and this comet would go over so many years and it would come again. Well, the story was handed down that the Crows put on their best regalia when they were expecting that comet. They were ready to die because they thought that comet was coming to cause the end of, the ultimate end of history. When it went by then they would undress, put their regalia away and they say, "Well we're all right for several more years. But how many, forty years, seventy years?" Things would be all right for that time. In my time they didn't do that, but I was told that in my grandmother's time and her mother's time the men would dress up in their regalia, real fine regalia, go out there and wait because they knew it was about the end of time. When it did come there was silence, everything was quiet, even the dogs were quiet. Nothing, just silence and it passed and when it passed, of course as it did and it must have, then they undressed and got their regular clothes on, got their fineries laid out, put them away for the next time in prayer. I mean they were in prayer while they were doing that and then right after they put their finery away and then gave the orders and then the women would go ahead and prepare something for them to eat. It was not a feast, but it was a special type of meal that they ate. It was broth, it was no feast, no big feast or anything but it was a kind of meditation type of thanksgiving or something that they took into themselves. That is what they did with the comet and they called it *Ihkachiishpishe*, it's got a tail, a Star With A Tail.

Comets are no longer feared by Crow people. They met the appearance of a rather bright and visible comet in the spring of 1996, Comet Hyakutake, with curiosity, wonder, and much discussion, not unlike their non-Crow neighbors.

In the past, meteor showers also brought fear. Inez described her grandmother's story of the great meteor shower of 1833—a shower so great that it caused most of the Plains Tribes, including the Crow, to name 1833 "The Year The Stars Fell":

There was a time that the stars in the universe all were moving in the skies at once. There were stars that came down even to the opening of the tipi, where the tipi poles are exposed at the top of the tipi. My grandmother told me about this. She said that they all cowered to the ground. I was told that they stayed there all night, and it was just before daylight before it quit. It was very unusual. The ground was all lit up as that was happening. It was very frightening I was told.

And Hanna explained the reaction of her grandmother to another meteor shower:

When stars fell out of heaven then they did something special, when they fell out of heaven they prayed, the women did. I remember my grandmother standing out there when the stars would fall, she would pray.

However, it is curious that shooting stars have never brought fear, they were simply seen as the movement of the star beings from one place in the sky to another. Carl recalled that in pre-reservation days the observation of a shooting star in the constellation of the Campsite Star, Corona Borealis, was a sign to move camp. Oscar, an elder from the St. Xavier area, expanded on this idea:

The Crow people are close to the things in the heavens. They say that the stars are places of abode, and that they sometimes move camp. The Caucasian says, "The star is falling." When the stars move camp like that, the Crow make wishes, such as, "I wish for a lot of money, horses." Things like that. Just as when the door of a house opens, one makes a wish, as we are told. They wish for a lot of money. I don't know if this philosophy is the same with Caucasians, but that is how it is with us Crow.

Fay, an elder from the Black Lodge District, summarized her knowledge of moving stars with firsthand experiences:

I know a little bit about the stars from what my father told me. Sometimes my father would go out in the night and he would look up at the stars and say, "Lots of stars, some are just changing places [shooting stars], but when there's too many, some come down to earth [meteors]. Both are very bright lights."

Up at Pryor one night my father saw a meteor and my uncle saw it too. It was quite a spectacle. They got up early the next morning to see what had happened. It was coming down to the earth at such a fast pace and it had a fire on the end of it, it was throwing out fire. It came down and it landed at Pryor Mountain. It left a very big round indent where it landed. Even today it is noticeable where this happened.

A couple days after it happened, we went with my father and uncle and saw it, but we were young then so we didn't care, we didn't know why it was important. This was at Lost Creek, and you can still see where the star came down; it had a tail that was fire and it really came at a fast pace. It landed with such a force that it left a big circular indentation in the land. It still remains there today at Lost Creek.

At one time it was said that the Star With A Tail [Halley's Comet] was going to fall and come to earth. They said, "It is coming to burn the earth." People heard about this and were terrified. They were told to put on their best clothes and not be caught unaware. "When you go to bed, be prepared," they said. My father put on his best clothes and stayed up by himself all night singing. After all this, they found out that it wasn't even true [laughs].

I saw it. The star came with such great light behind it. Here was the star—on the back end, way back here was this light [using Plains Indian sign language she indicates a star with her right hand and a fire with her left hand, arms stretched out to indicate the distance]. One night it appeared. Everyone must have seen it because it was so far up in the heavens. As it went, the fire was behind it [she indicates a great length with her arm]. People saw this and they went to pray with sweetgrass, making good wishes. We don't know what happened to it since it passed the earth. The earth didn't burn up, so we don't know what happened to it. I was maybe about five years old at the time [she was born in 1905].

THE NORTHERN LIGHTS

Another nighttime phenomenon that is often observed after sweats or during Native American Church meetings is the appearance of the Northern Lights. Although the Crow have a name for them, *awáxkowaasaashiia*, "lights shining from the sky," they have no specific stories about their origin, but they are often watched for their beauty and magnitude. Hanna explained:

> The Aurora Borealis, or Northern Lights, we call them *awáxkowaasaashiia*, lights from the sky, from the atmosphere. Sometimes, you can see things in those lights, like tipis and fires, they are red and blue and white. Sometimes when they come they shoot up, they shoot up over you and there is a sound, it goes over you and you can hear—shshshsh—sometimes. And they say it is going to be cold.

Comets, meteors, and the Aurora Borealis are all well known to Crow people. And, just as for all peoples, their appearances incite much comment.

Chapter 9

THE SUN, THE MOON, AND THE MILKY WAY

THE SUN AND THE MOON

To the Crow people the sun is seen as a male and is called *Isáahkax-aalia*, "Old Man," and the moon is considered a female and is known as *Káalixaalia*, "Old Woman." These two heavenly bodies hold special importance and are observed carefully throughout the entire year. The elder Lloyd explained how the identity of these two sacred beings was revealed to the Crow:

> Here's the story about why they call the sun the Old Man. See, they relate to the heavenly bodies, the sun is life to them—life, everything. They say, all living things are dependent upon that sun. For warmth, all living things need that sun. The light and that kind of thing. So with that, they observed with reverence and appreciation. That's the closest I can come to on that. So, why they call the sun the Old Man? They say during an eclipse, this is so far back, we don't know, long time ago, probably legendary times. They say that during that eclipse the sun and the moon crossed over. They looked up there to observe this phenomenon, an eclipse. They say the sun was an old man, he'd been up there for so long that he's an old man. And the moon was an old lady.

That's why they refer to the moon as the Old Lady, *Káalixaalia*, our grandmother. Our grandfather, the Old Man. Just like they say *bilísaahke* [water old man], water is also referred to as grandfather. Land is referred to as our mother, our first mother, because it gives life, it provides all your needs. That's why they refer to it as Mother Earth, *Awaisahké* [Earth Mother].

When an eclipse did occur, the Crow felt it was a bad omen, a time when the sun had momentarily died. Raelynn, an elder from the Black Lodge area, explained some of the feelings associated with these celestial events:

When the moon crossed in front of the sun, caused an eclipse you know, they would say, "*Axxaashe shée*—the sun has died," they thought it was bad, a time of happenings, they said. They would have to fast about it and look after things because they thought that was telling that it wasn't good, it wasn't well what would come. Not until some time had passed did they begin to feel at ease again.

The sun and moon are constant and move in concert with each other. It is understandable that a break in that constant, seemingly predictable movement—such as with an eclipse—causes discomfort.

As a matter of practicality, the sun is used to predict the weather and to tell time. Hanna, from Ft. Smith, explained what she had been taught:

Anything that I give you is just from the elders telling it to me when I was a girl. Now the sun, they know the sun. When the sun sets they used to say, "It must be nice and warm, you see he's got his many colored robe on," or, "It must be cold because he has the gray robe." The sun, he covers up when he goes to bed.

They use to say that he has many colored robes, red robe or orange, whatever it might be *hisshishipite* [dark red] or *hiitchikaate* [pink] or stuff like that, the sun had many robes. Also, they can tell time by the sun too as it goes over, by the shadows they just know when noon is, sunrise and sunset and between that time they can regulate the time from the sun too.

The daily movement of the sun across the sky, on a path called the ecliptic, is termed *baaanníile* and the movement, left to right, is considered sacred. Thus when one enters a tipi, a sweatlodge, a Sun Dance arbor, or any other sacred structure, one turns to the left and circles around to the right. And upon leaving a tipi in the morning, one takes four steps out of the door and then turns to the right, once again following the path of the sun.

In meetings of the Native American Church a large crescent moon made of sand is built in the center of the tipi. From one tip to the other a line is drawn along its crest. This line is said to represent the life of a Native American Church adherent. This line is referred to as the "road of life" in English and in the Crow language it is called *annii-leeche*, literally the "animate route," or *baaanniile*, the "path of the sun"; both are understood as the road of life.

The position of sunrise is also utilized to set the position of doorways. The tipi erected for meetings of the Native American Church is set so the doorway is aligned with a peg placed in the ground at sunrise of that morning. Doorways to Sun Dance arbors are similarly positioned, so that the first morning rays of the sun will strike the center pole with their light.

The four significant positions of the sun throughout the year—summer solstice, fall equinox, winter solstice, and spring equinox—also hold special importance. The equinoxes are ritually signified with the first splashes of water in the sweatlodge. Sun Dances are held on the summer solstice, which is termed *axxaashe biiwuukusshiia*, "when the sun turns to the right." The winter solstice, called *axxaashe aliikusshiia*, "when the sun turns to the left," is a time of social and religious significance. It is then that the social winter dances are held by the reservation districts. It is also the time to begin the first of the four preliminary Sun Dance bundle openings which lead to the next summer's Sun Dances. As George, an elder from the Reno District, explained:

> A person who wants to sponsor a Sun Dance must give tobacco and gifts to a Sun Dance Chief. After this is done then a medicine bundle ceremony is held in mid-winter, during the shortest day of the year. This day is known as *Axxaashe Aliikusshiia*, the returning of the sun. During this ceremony the sponsor announces his intentions of sponsoring a Sun Dance that summer. Then the Sun Dance bundles are opened, songs sung, and a feast is given.

The moon is also utilized for determining when medicine bundles can be opened. In fact, Sun Dance bundle openings are often called "Full Moon Meetings." Family medicine bundles are often opened on full or new moons. The new moon is thought of as symbolizing growth, since subsequent days will show a steady increase in its growth until it is full. For this reason medicine bundles are opened at this time and children are encouraged to jump into the air, so as to receive the growth symbolized by the developing moon. Hanna, an elder from Ft. Smith, related this idea to the maturing of berries:

> Another thing that my grandmother always said was that the moon is the one that ripens the berries. After the sun puts its sweat into that fruit, the moon agitates it to ripen overnight so you can go out there before the sun comes out and they'll be ripe, she said. She believed it, I mean this is what she believed and this is what she found out to be true because she was always at those places very early in the day.

The moon is also observed to predict the weather in the coming month. The first crescent of a waxing moon is observed to see its relative position to the horizon. The further the points of the crescent are pointing up or away from the horizon, the more severe will be the oncoming weather. But the opposite, the points of the crescent towards the earth, means good weather. The difference is often determined by holding a stick or other straight edge across the crescent to determine its angle in relation to the horizon. Indistinct first crescents, ones that point neither to nor away from the horizon, can lead to much discussion, even heated arguments. In explaining the significance of a rising new moon, Raelynn, an elder from Black Lodge stated:

> When it's on its back, the wind is blowing through, so that's cold weather. When it's standing, it's warming its back, so that's good weather.

The moon is thought to control not only the weather but human reproduction as well. The Crow say that there are ten lunar months from the time of conception to birth. For this reason the number ten holds special significance for the Crow. As Jake, an elder from Black Lodge, expressed it:

> The white man says there are nine months until a baby is born, but the Indian says there are ten months from conception to birth. If you count the moons from conception to birth, it's ten months.

Oscar, an elder from the Big Horn District, alluded to both beliefs about the moon:

> The Old Woman, the moon, takes the water and the clouds and puts them into motion. As we think upon the way the women have their monthly cycles, we ought to realize something from this.

Since the Crow believe the moon to be a benevolent old woman who takes good care of the humans she "adopts," she is highly sought as a spiritual helper by both women and men. The concept of the moon as an old woman is reinforced by the Crow belief that the dark areas on the face of the moon is an old woman hanging up meat to dry. Raelynn, an elder from the Two Leggings area in Black Lodge, explained this idea when she defined the address term for the moon:

> The moon is the one that rules the night, when you talk to her you call her *Káalixaalia*, very old, ancient woman, and they say there's a woman in the moon, in the shadow of the moon I mean, hanging up meat to dry. The moon is the one that rules the night.

Carl, an elder from Big Horn, provided the following description of how the sun and moon are important and used by the Crow:

The moon is very much a part of our lives, the moon, the grandmother. We make reference to her in worship. We acknowledge the moon as a grandma. "Show us the good signs, show us the good way," we say that. I don't know about others, but in our way of worship we refer to the moon as grandmother. And then we say my grandfather is the sun, my grandmother is the moon, they're living beings.

When there's a new moon, the old timers would look up and say, "*Aa* [yes], it's a good one, coming up just right, *chíleeitcheek* [it's rising good], getting up just right." Other times they say, "It's coming back with a lot of water," [when the end points of the crescent are pointing up] which means a lot of weather until the next month. If it shows up real good, it's going to be pleasant, and in that sense it is making a prediction, "I'm going to have a good month, I'm going to have a trying month." And particularly when they're going on a war party or they're going on a vision quest, they watch for that sign and govern themselves accordingly.

When you're little they say, "It's a new moon. Come on out, come on out." Just when it's beginning to shape, they told you and you would do it, you would jump and say, "By the next moon, I'll be this tall." You'd keep doing that, it's part of a little ritual we do. We don't worship it, but we know what we are looking at, and we just go out and say, "*Bilítaachiiakala chiléek,*" [the moon is rising now] it's coming back up now, it's getting up. *Iipíishile bilíchile kammiihíliakeek* [The next new moon I'll be this tall]. And then we just jump up and down.

I have a grandson who lives in Colorado and he's four now, and a woman criticized my daughter and said, "Your son should be in school, he shouldn't be around the mall with you." She said, "He's not old enough." She said, "How old is he?" She said, "Four." She said, "He looks like a six year old or older." She said, "How come you're so big?" He said, "Because I jump when the moon comes up." It probably meant nothing to that woman, but he does it religiously.

Then when you see sun dogs, they take that as a sign of a change in the weather. That there's going to be heat coming if there are no bright sun dogs, you just see that little speck. But when it's a broad one, like a halo, then they say cold is coming. A halo around the moon is the same thing. And then when you get a sun dog you say, "This is going to be a good time to do the stealth things, to sneak up on an enemy, take what we want." But when it's real clear, "If we do it, we're going to be vulnerable."

It's also a sign of fertility. Women, when they're pregnant, see a sun dog then they're going to have an easy childbirth. When you see a sun dog you say, "I can't put off what I was going to do," you got to do it. It's time for me to make a decision, a significant move.

The sun and moon, and their appearances and positions, provide vital information to the Crow.

THE MILKY WAY

The Milky Way is perceived as a trail which was created when Old Man Coyote, the Crow culture-hero, ran away with a woman. The Crow term for this feature of the night is *Ammíaaalaau*, "Where They Take Women," in remembrance of the incident which created it. The following version was told by Ethan, an elder from the Black Lodge area:

> *Ammíaaalaau* [Where They Take Women], there's a story about Old Man Coyote associated with that. You know he was very lecherous. Well, they say that one time he came to a camp at night and stole a man's wife. Instead of running off to a motel [laughs] you know, he took her to the sky. But as they ran, they left a trail of stars. That same evening the husband found that his wife was gone. The whole camp searched until somebody noticed the trail in the sky. They followed it and found them. The man punched Old Man Coyote and took his wife back [laughing].

The position of the Milky Way in the sky is seen as an indicator of clear or stormy weather. One elder stated, "In the winter when we can see *Ammíaaalaau* in the northwest, then we know it is going to be good weather." Inez, an elder from the Lodge Grass area, elaborated on this concept:

> You can tell people about *Ammíaaalaau*, "Where They Take Women," or the Milky Way. On a night when there are many clouds, very cloudy, you can go outside and say something like, "*Ammíaaalaau* is north of us" or "*Ammíaaalaau* is along the top of the mountains" and the clouds will break up. Stand to the Milky Way and repeat this and they will break up for you.

The Milky Way, the moon, and the sun provide clues to weather and nature, and religious beliefs and practices—they provide both natural and supernatural teachings. The Crow people have learned how to live with them and amongst them.

Chapter 10

IN THE COMPANY
OF STARS

As we have seen, for the Crow the stars have provided an understanding of the forces of nature, its cycles, and the place of their people within them. When this tribe began its long journey into becoming a distinct people, they were led by a man with a vision of the stars. These visions guided the Crow people to the proper place for them to live, in the landscape known today as Montana and Wyoming. There, in a fourth and final fast, their leader, No Intestines, saw the stars transformed as Sacred Tobacco seeds. These seeds appeared as sparkling stars at the base of the mountain which stood at the center of their new world.

Throughout this trek to their homeland and their subsequent movements to protect and explore and hunt within their historic territory, the Crow kept careful watch of the entire world all about them. This awareness drew in the sky and they gleaned what information they could about its regularities and incorporated this knowledge into their everyday lives. The movements and actions of the stars, the sun, the moon, and the motions of the planets, as well as the appearances of shooting stars, comets, and meteor showers, provided Crow people with concepts and principles by which to live. It can be said that the very survival of the Crow people relied upon their knowledge of when

Sign posted by the National Park Service on the road leaving Ft. Smith, Big Horn District (photo by Doug Kuhlman).

the seasons changed and, in turn, when plants or animals should be harvested and hunted. This knowledge was in large part provided by the regular motions of the beings of the sky.

The practical aspects of food acquisition and sequential camp movements were certainly aided by the information acquired from the sky. Just as importantly, however, is how the cycles of the sky provided and continue to serve the spiritual and moral needs of the Crow people. Crow behaviors, practices, values, and ethics are based on the beliefs and philosophies of the origins and organization of the universe. Therefore, for the Crow, the complex set of relationships that keeps them intact as a people has evolved from the sacred motions and appearances of the cosmos.

From childhood, when jumping at the new moon to promote growth, to adolescence, when learning proper men's and women's roles with star stories, through adulthood, when one polishes the skills and remembers the moral and ethical precepts learned from those ones above, until old age, when one turns to instruct those who are younger, a Crow person looks up to read messages and signs given long ago but still relevant today.

A Crow cannot take a sweat, nurture a child, care properly for a relative, engage in ritual, create art, discuss philosophy, or tell cosmic time without some knowledge of the stars. Incremental phases of the night, as well as seasons of the whole year, are all defined in the sky. Predictive knowledge of immediate and distant weather may be learned from these celestial bodies. The nightly, seasonal, yearly, and infinite turnings in the celestial sphere all provide a richness of knowledge to the trained eyes of the Crow.

This Crow interconnectedness with the heavens was powerfully evoked for me one morning when my Crow father, Guy White Clay, reminisced about his service in the military. He had been a tail gunner on a B-29 Superfortress in the Pacific Theater at the end of World War II. On one mission, when returning from a high-altitude night bombing strike over the Japanese home islands, he was watching the clear night from his seat in the rear of the plane. Then he saw the stars passing above and their reflection skimming along the calm ocean below. At that moment, he told me, he said to himself, "*Ihkaxáaxaaheetak Ihké aléwahkuua, aho, aho*—The stars are sparkling. The stars we know, thanks, thanks."

APPENDIX
CROW STAR NAMES OF
UNIDENTIFIED CONSTELLATIONS

The names of two Crow constellations were provided by three elders, but exactly which constellations were being referred to could not be determined. The first one was *Ihkaiishbíia*, "Cougar or Mountain Lion Star." Two elders, Debra and Ethan, knew this name but neither had ever seen the constellation nor could offer stories relating to it. The second constellation was referred to as *Báakkaalaakkokaashe*, "Snapping Turtle Above." Debra knew the name of this constellation and remembered its origin story:

The Turtle Up Above, my mother told me at one time why there was a turtle in the sky. There was a camp being attacked by another tribe, they were slaughtering the camp. There was two kids, a little boy and girl that was running away from the camp to the river the camp, as that camp was being slaughtered and there was a *dáakkokaashe* [snapping turtle] they say. This *dáakkokaashe* said, "Come and get on me, I will take you up there away from the camp." And they both got on the turtle and went up river. As they were going up the river it seem like they were going up in the sky and when they finally looked down they were up in the sky and turtle said, "This is where we are going to be. And when your relatives, your people pray to you, then you look upon them people and whatever they ask you can give to them." In that way we get help from this *Báakkaalaakkokaashe* and them two, the little boy and girl. In some ways, miracle ways, if you are sick you pray that you get well to these stars and that Turtle Up Above is praying for you as well

111

as them two little boys and girls are praying for the Crow Indian people. That's how it was told to me when I was a little girl and that's why they say there is a turtle up there. I use to get up and would look for it but I still can't find where it is, but it is up there and that's what my mother was telling me.

FURTHER READING

This book is based on my observations and the narratives of contemporary Crow people. Originally written purposely to show the vitality of Crow culture to students at the tribally controlled college, Little Big Horn College, it presents more detail than previously available to the general public. However, many previous works on or about Crow people contain star knowledge, and these sources are outlined below.

Curtis, Edward S.
1980   The Apsaroke and Hidatsa. In volume four of *The North American Indian*. Johnson Reprint Corporation. New York, NY.

   This classic Crow ethnography contains a version of the Seven Brothers story (pages 117–126).

Davis, Leslie (editor)
1979   Lifeways of the Intermontane and Plains Montana Indians. *Museum of the Rockies Occasional Papers* 1:43–56.

   Included in this series of articles is one written and illustrated by Crow tribal member and historian, Max Big Man. This unique description of the Crow Tobacco Society's adoption and membership (Beaver) dances includes drawings of Star Chapter members.

Fitzgerald, Michael O.
1991   *Yellowtail: Crow Medicine Man and Sun Dance Chief*. University of Oklahoma Press. Norman, OK.

This biography of a Crow Sun Dance leader includes descriptions of the significance of the sweatlodge (pages 106–110), a version of the Seven Bulls story (pages 110–113), and how this elder greeted the stars (page 113). The book also contains much more information about Crow spirituality and personal anecdotes of the elder Tom Yellowtail.

Frey, Rodney
1987   *The World of the Crow Indians, As Driftwood Lodges*. University of Oklahoma Press. Norman, OK.

This book provides an insightful view of contemporary Crow culture, including a detailed description of the clan relationships and the worldview as reflected through the present day Shoshone-Crow Sun Dance.

Linderman, Frank B.
1931   *Old Man Coyote*. John Day Company. New York, NY.

This book contains several stories of the Crow people including the Twins (pages 109–130), the Seven Brothers (pages 137–166), and Old Woman's Grandson (pages 207–254).

Lowie, Robert H.
1993   *Myths and Traditions of the Crow Indians*. Bison Books, University of Nebraska Press. Lincoln, NE.

This extensive compilation of Crow stories includes a number of stories dealing with stars and star knowledge including Old Woman's Grandson (pages 52–73), the Twins (pages 74–98), the Seven Bulls (pages 161–164), the Seven Brothers (pages 204–211), as well as others.

1919   The Tobacco Society of the Crow Indians. *Anthropological Papers of the American Museum of Natural History* 21(2): 101–200.

This ethnographic overview of the Crow's Sacred Tobacco Society includes a description of the society's star origins (pages 176–189), and the use of a stick to point at the stars and the Tobacco (page 175).

1922   The Religion of the Crow Indians. *Anthropological Papers of the American Museum of Natural History* 25(2): 309–444.

Included in this description of Crow religion is information on Crow beliefs associated with the sun, moon, Big Dipper, Morning Star, and stars in general (pages 318–322), and the importance of stars in the sweatlodge (pages 426–431).

1956   *The Crow Indians*. Holt, Rinehart and Winston. New York, NY.

This historic ethnography about Crow people contains many references to stars in religious beliefs and practices, and a version of the Old Woman's Grandson story (pages 134–157).

Nabokov, Peter

1970   *Two Leggings: The Making of a Crow Indian*. Thomas
Crowell Company. New York, NY.

This unique biography of a Crow man in the time of the buffalo days
has many references to Crow beliefs and practices, including a brief
description of the star sweatlodge way (page 24), and a prayer to the
stars (page 94).

1988   *Cultivating Themselves: The Inter-play of Crow Indian Religion
and History*. Ph.D. dissertation, University of California. Berkeley,
CA.

This exhaustive ethnography on the Crow's Tobacco Society includes
descriptions of the star origins of the society and star imagery in the
society's artwork.

Old Coyote, Henry D.
1980   *Isshiiooshkunnaalaau*. Bilingual Materials Development Center.
Crow Agency, MT.

This bilingual version of the Seven Brothers written by a
well-respected elder is probably the best published version of this
popular story.

Real Bird, Henry
1990   *The Creation Story of the Crow People*. MA thesis, Eastern Montana
College. Billings MT.

This master's thesis written by a Crow tribal member includes a variant of the Old Woman's Grandson narrative sprinkled throughout
the text.

Simms, Stephen C.
1903   *Traditions of the Crows*. Field Museum of Natural History. Chicago,
IL.

This short compilation of Crow stories includes a version of the
Seven Bulls (pages 301–302), the Twins (pages 303–306), and the
Seven Brothers (pages 309–311).

Voget, Fred W.
1984   *The Shoshoni-Crow Sun Dance*. University of Oklahoma Press. Norman, OK.

Through this well-researched and intuitive ethnographic work on the
contemporary Crow Sun Dance, the importance and use of the stars
in the Sun Dance are presented (pages 81–82, 299–304, 232–234).

Wildschut, William, and John C. Ewers
1975   *Crow Indian Medicine Bundles*. Contributions from the Museum of
the American Indian, Heye Foundation. New York, NY.

This interesting volume on Crow medicine bundles is based on the
field notes of the collector William Wildschut. Included in the intro-
duction is a description of the interrelatedness of cosmic phenomena

and Crow religion (pages 1–3). In addition, many of the medicine bundles described in the text derive from the sun, moon, and stars.

Williamson, Ray A., and Claire R. Farrer (editors)
1992   *Earth and Sky: Visions of the Cosmos in Native American Folklore.* University of New Mexico Press. Albuquerque, NM.

This introductory volume on ethnoastronomy presents information about this developing area of the human sciences and includes a series of articles on aspects of the ethnoastronomy of various North American Indian groups.

STUDY GUIDE

prepared by Claire R. Farrer
California State University, Chico

Page xii

Farrer uses the word "Indian," which is a misnomer from the mistake made by Columbus over 500 years ago when he thought he had discovered the outliers of the Indies. Other terms used for the indigenous people of the Americas include "Native American," "American Indian," "Native," and the Canadian term that is gaining in popularity, "First Nations People." Each of these terms carries a particular set of baggage. What do they mean to you?

Pages xiv–xv

How do you keep track of time? What do you know of your own calendar? Are you familiar with any other calendars, such as the Chinese one? What ways did Indian people in your area keep their own calendars?

For more information on the complicated business of solar and lunar calendars and commensuration, the process of adjusting one to fit the other, see the introductory chapters to both of the Williamson books cited in the Foreword.

Page xv

Narratives are known to be true by people of the culture producing them. Yet outsiders construct typologies—organizational schemes—like Farrer presents here with myth, legend, and tale. Is this justifiable when the people themselves make no such determinations?

Page 1

All people have names for themselves. Often these names translate into English as "The People" or "Human Beings." By what terms do you distinguish yourself? How do your names for yourself differentiate you from others? Why is it important to do this? What about your surname? Why is that important and why is it usually the father's rather than the mother's name that is used? Do you know of anyone who uses the mother's name as a surname?

Page 2

Before the coming of the "Whiteman," as non-Indians are often termed, how do you suppose Crow people knew when the seasons were to change? Do you think they waited for the plants of a season to declare that season had begun? Why?

Page 3

McCleary identifies three primary groups of Crow people who also considered themselves to be part of a larger Crow identity. What are the divisions you recognize in your life beyond your family?

   At the bottom of the page, McCleary notes that "The mountains remain a vital resource to Crow people for food, medicines, and spiritual retreat." Natural medicines, derived from plant fruits and leaves, roots, barks, and sometimes even earths, are important to all Native people and increasingly important to non-Indians as well who practice "alternative" medicine. To what does the alternative refer? What are your experiences with alternative medicines? Who told you of them—parents, friends, grandparents, knowledgeable people in the local community? Why do you trust them?

Page 4

Crow people cooperate with the National Park Service to allow visitors to visit the historical site of Custer's last battle. Why would Indian people be interested in maintaining the site of Custer's last stand?

Page 7

Anthropologists note matrilineal and patrilineal systems of kinship, among others. In a matrilineal system, one's "blood" kin are only those one acquires through a relationship to one's mother: e.g., mother's mother and her descendants, mother's sister and her descendants. When people recognize "blood" kin as being those with whom they can trace a genetic link through both parents, the people are said to have a bilateral kinship system; this is the primary mode of kinship in the contemporary United States.

Draw your own bilateral kinship chart. Then color in only those people to whom you are related through your mother. In a matrilineal system these would be your blood kin; oftentimes, in such a system, you would not be considered to be related at all to those people through your father.

Draw your own bilateral kinship chart. Then color in only those people to whom you are related through your father. In a patrilineal system these would be your blood kin; oftentimes, in such a system, you would not be considered to be related at all to those people through your mother.

Now that you have played with matrilineal, patrilineal, and bilateral kinship, how would you characterize the Crow view of kinship?

Pages 7 and 8

"Clan fathers" and "clan mothers" are special terms Crow people use to distinguish important people related to them through their father's side of a family. Do you know of any equivalents to these positions in contemporary United States culture?

Page 8

McCleary provides the gloss for *ahó* as being "thanks." Which part of the phrase *ihkaxáaxaaheete* do you suppose means star/stars? Keep this phrase handy as you continue to read and see if you can determine the word for star before it is given in the text.

Page 9

In Anglo—a word Indian people sometimes use to mean those who are not Indian and not African-American—society it is important to classify and divide things into such categories as anthropology or astronomy or physics or mathematics. The term anthropologists use for those who divide things up is "compartmentalization." Try to imagine your world if there were no such compartmentalization but rather everything holistic (the contrast term). How would you refer to music? To science? Indeed, is it important to make such reference? What is the cosmovision of those who live in the United States? Is there more than one in existence?

Page 10

Performances are keyed, or recognized, by many different markers. If for example, someone says to you, "You look great," there are many different ways you could interpret the statement: "You look great?" "You look great!" "You *look* great." "*You* look great." We know what is meant partially by how the statement is performed. How do you recognize more stylized and formal performances of, say, a speech, a report of information, a report of a tragedy, a recitation, an untrue story, and so on?

There are clues on page 10 about the part of the phrase on page 8 that means star. Did you spot them?

Page 11

Are there particular markers of performance that you and your friends use? That are used in your family? How do you know you are hearing a political speech rather than an historical one? What are the differences between written reports of oral events and the actual oral events themselves?

Why, do you suppose, Westerners insist on only one truth? Similarly, why, do you suppose, non-Westerners maintain there is truth in every rendition of a story?

Page 12

It is here that McCleary first tells readers that the word for star, in Crow, is *ihké*. Had you already figured it out? The technique of isolating parts of words or phrases into their constituent meanings is one of the skills utilized by linguists and linguistic anthropologists when they are first trying to learn an unwritten language or a language they have never heard before. How many parts are there to the word "parts"? If you responded two, you are correct. "Part" has meaning on its own and, while "s" does not have a meaning as a separate word, native speakers of English recognize it as a meaningful unit nonetheless, since adding it to a word makes the word move from a state of singularity to one of plurality. Not all languages form plurals in this fashion, but the comparison and word attack technique is useful to help a person to begin to understand a language different from her/his own.

Page 16

In Western cultures, the zodiacal constellations, in particular, are also the subject of many stories. If you don't know them already, use your library to look up information on Taurus and Scorpio, in the zodiac, or Orion and Andromeda as examples of non-zodiacal constellations. Are these stories literally true or are they to be understood as metaphors?

Pages 16–18

Some Western scholars have difficulty accepting the oral traditions of non-Western people. Western history is based upon documents and accounts—sometimes written by those present at the event but often written by those who heard of it or who reported on it second, or even third, hand. Because Westerners rely on writing and, therefore, have forgotten how to remember, they are generally skeptical of those whose memories hold the equivalent of encyclopedias. Nonetheless, all history is a reconstruction, it is constructed from sources each culture believes to be valid. How is recent history constructed? For example, what do you know of Elvis Presley and how do you know it? Or, how do you know of the Vietnam war that engaged so much American energy in the 60s and 70s? Similarly, what are your sources for understanding the recent presidential election? What is valid history for you?

Page 19

Western people have a saying, "Red sky at night, sailors' delight; red sky at morning, sailors take warning." What does this mean? How does it relate to the Crow perception of sunset colors?

Page 23

Simultaneously existing versions of narratives are commonplace among people the world over whose cultures are carried primarily orally. Even among cultures that utilize writing, when people write what had been an oral story, multiple versions exist. Consider the stories of Jesus Christ in the New Testament Gospels of Matthew, Mark, Luke, and John. While purporting to tell the same story, there are significant differences among the versions. What is there in your life that produces different versions of the same event?

Pages 24–29

In Western science, those stars that are high in the sky, close to the pole star, Polaris, are called circumpolar, literally—"around with the pole." In the Western tradition, circumpolar stars do not set; indeed, that belief is often included in the definition of a circumpolar star or constellation. However, mountainous horizons provide ways for circumpolar stars and constellations to disappear, to set, during the course of a night. Nonetheless, Westerners persist in their definition of circumpolar.

Here is a method of locating the North Star; it assumes you are at 40° North Latitude. Go outside after dark and face north. Stretch your arms out in front of you then bring them together and turn your wrists so that your palms are toward your face. Tuck in your thumbs and place one hand atop the other, with the bottom hand resting on the horizon; your hands now mark off about 40°. Look for the star that is just above your hand; it should be Polaris, the North Star. (Adjustments in this method can be made for various latitudes: one hand describes approximately 20° while one hand and two fingers of the other yield approximately 30°.)

Perhaps the best known circumpolar constellation is that of the Big Dipper, itself a part of a larger constellation called Ursa Major, or the Great Bear. The bowl and handle of the Big Dipper are often utilized to provide both short- and long-term clocks. Let us hold the time constant at midnight and always have reference to the North Star, Polaris in our era. On the Summer Solstice (around June 21) the open top of the bowl of the Big Dipper will be to the left of the North Star with the handle pointing upward, toward the north. On the Autumn Equinox (around September 21) the open bowl of the Big Dipper will be below the North Star and the handle will be pointing upward to the left, roughly west-northwest. On the Winter Solstice (around December 21) the open bowl of the Big Dipper will be on the right side of the North Star and the handle will be pointing below the North Star, to the south. On the Vernal Equinox (around March 21) the open bowl of the Big Dipper will be above the North Star while the handle will be on the right side of the North Star and pointing downward, roughly east-southeast.

The Big Dipper can be observed to move 15° each hour of the night. On a nightly basis, it takes 23 hours and 56 minutes for the Big Dipper to return to its previous position. This four-minute lag time each night accumulates into the differences in the appearance of the Big Dipper throughout a solar year. The 15° of movement each night is quite easily visible to the naked eye, as, for that matter, is 71/2° of movement that marks out half hours throughout the night.

Go out on a clear night, well away from city lights (or look through two of the cardboard rolls inside paper towels or toilet tissue rolls to cut out ambient light.) Locate the Big Dipper and watch its movements over the course of a couple of hours. Once you have seen the movement for yourself, it will be much easier to understand how the Crow, and other Indian people, use the sky to provide both clocks and seasonal markers.

Page 26

The Native American Church is one that crosses Indian tribal boundaries. Although it is hundreds of years old, and although there is the Native American Religious Freedom Act, members of the Native American Church are still persecuted and prosecuted in this country for following their beliefs. One of the sacraments of the Native American Church is the use of peyote under very stringent conditions; yet many see this as drug use and condemn the Church for its practice. Similarly, some fundamental Protestants condemn Roman Catholics for their use of wine, also a drug, in a sacrament. What is the difference between drug usage in sacramental conditions and drug use in general? Is the use of drugs in religious ritual justifiable?

Page 28

If you are not already familiar with it, find a copy of the *Farmer's Almanac*. Note the use of stars and weather signs to predict both weather and when to plant which crops. Have you, in your own experience, heard anyone refer to the stars as signs of what is to come? Have you ever read your Horoscope in a newspaper? If the answer to either of these questions is yes, you have more in common with the Crow than you might have imagined.

Page 32

McCleary writes, "The Crow believe that the strongest communications with the supernatural occur through dreams or visions which take place during the 'dark face time.'" When is it that your people believe the strongest communications occur with the supernatural?

Page 37

Many Native American Indians believe that the proper ones to raise children are grandparents. Parents are often perceived as being too sexually active and too busy making a living to be effective teachers of the young. Therefore, many groups deem it a high honor when a child is raised by grandparents. This practice of fostering a child is common to Native people. What are the differences between this kind of fostering and the Anglo term of a foster child?

Determining the sex of an unborn child, before sonograms were commonplace, was an activity that people throughout the world engaged in. Have you heard of ways of predicting the sex of an unborn child?

Page 40

What happens to religious tradition or ritual when the sacred place for such a tradition or ritual ceases to be?

Page 42

Is your family rooted in place? Why? Why not? What feelings and stories were communicated to you by your family about your roots? Were these roots tied to a place?

Page 43

Venus is so bright in the sky, whether it appears helically before sunrise or after sunset, that it has excited interest from virtually every Native group of people. The Maya even constructed artificial points over which to view the rise of Venus and even oriented a building at Uxmal in the Yucatan out of alignment with the other buildings in the city in order to have a proper Venus observatory. Ray Williamson in *Living the Sky*, pages 47–48, provides perhaps the easiest to understand explanation of Venus's movement through the sky:

> . . . Venus [as both] Morning Star and Evening Star were intently observed by most Native American cultures and were sometimes used to time important ceremonies . . . Venus first appears as an evening star just east of the sun a few minutes after the disk of the sun has slipped below the horizon. From then on, each night it moves farther and farther away from the sun and becomes brighter and brighter. About a month before Venus reaches its eastern extreme from the sun, it attains its maximum brightness. A full 132 days after its first appearance, Venus again begins to more toward the sun (that is, the angle between the sun and Venus begins to close). . . . After approximately 263 days (the exact number depends greatly on an individual's visual acuity and the state of the atmosphere), the evening star disappears in the consuming brightness of the sun's disk. Eight days later, it reappears as a morning star, a position it maintains for approximately 263 days. Its reappearance as an evening star requires 46 to 70 days, depending again on the condition of the atmosphere and the visual acuity of the observer. The entire synodic cycle takes 584 days, or eight–fifths of a year.

Ask the assistance of a local astronomy club, or a professional or amateur astronomer, to locate Venus in your home area. Then watch it weekly at the same time of day or night to begin to comprehend its cycling. The cycle is a complex one that, as Williamson notes, takes 584 days to complete. This tells us that Native American star gazers were astute observers and patient ones as well.

Page 45

Again, enlist the aid of an astronomer to help you locate Mars. It is easily recognizable by its reddish color. How long is its cycle? Where in the heavens can it be viewed by earth-dwelling people?

Page 49

Most bookstores carry very inexpensive star charts. Following the instructions included with them, locate the stars McCleary mentions in order to recognize the Crow Hand Star constellation.

The sweatlodge has become popular with ersatz Indians and so-called New Agers. In American Indian traditions, the sweatlodge is a place for purification and healing. What have you heard of sweatlodge ceremonies in your area?

Pages 51–57 and 57–62

These long narratives contain moral lessons. How many of them can you identify?

Page 64

Yellow Leggings can be called a culture hero, in that he brought important aspects of life to the Crow. Who are American culture heroes? Are there any culture heroines?

Were-animals seem to have a place in the narratives of most people of the world. What were-animals are familiar to you through your culture's narratives? How about the animals associated with vampires and/or Halloween?

Pages 65–71 and 71–73

Narratives such as these contain vast amounts of cultural information, often coded in metaphors and allusions. What ways does your culture communicate similar information? Do Disney films accomplish some of the same goals as narratives such as these? Why or why not?

Pages 74 and 75

From what you have learned of stars and constellations, why do you think the Crow construct four stages of time and know the world to be composed of four elements?

Page 77

Is knowledge "owned" in non-Indian culture? How about medical knowledge? What is considered to be personal property in United States mainstream culture? Could religion or ritual be personal property to an average, non-Indian American?

Page 80

Crow adoption, as with many other American Indian tribes, is accomplished for somewhat different reasons than is adoption in mainstream American culture. If a family has a surfeit of children yet relatives of one of the parents have no or only a few children, it is a relatively easy matter for biological parents "to give a child" to the child-impoverished household. The child so given grows up knowing who its biological parents are but also knows the act of love and sacrifice it took for it to be given to another household. In older times, children were often adopted-out for a period of time so that a child could learn the language of another tribe; these were usually exchanges between tribes so they could learn each other's languages. Such adoptions also assured that war would not be pursued, as no one wishes to go to war when their own children are with the other camp. How is adoption viewed in your family?

Chapter 7

On page 94, McCleary notes, " . . . gifts from the stars have given the Crow a means of survival—a way of life." Are there any similar stories that give a way of life among your people?

Pages 95–97

What do meteors and comets mean in contemporary American culture? What did they, and especially Halley's comet, portend in the past? What was the significance of the impact of the meteor "pearls" that recently slammed into Jupiter and was "visible" on the internet and television as well as through telescopes?

Page 97

Why does McCleary distinguish between comets and meteors? How are they alike? How are they different?

Page 98

Throughout this book, McCleary has looked to "elders" for knowledge. What position do elders hold in contemporary mainstream American culture?

Page 103

A solstice is when the sun appears to stand still on the horizon, rising and setting in the same position for several days in a row rather than moving its position daily against a horizon, as during the rest of the year. An equinox is when the hours of daylight and dark are approximately equal. It is much easier to see a solstice than it is to determine an equinox. What events occur around solstices and equinoxes in your culture's practices?

Page 104

People around the world ascribe particular visual meanings to the dark patches visible on the moon. What stories did you hear growing up concerning these dark places?

Page 106

Coyote, or other animals among other tribes, is a creature who teaches how to behave by breaking every proper rule of social conduct. He is often seen as a funny character, because he is so outrageous. What animal, or mythical person, serves a similar function in your culture?

Page 107

The stars are of vital importance in Crow culture. What in your culture assumes similar importance?